What Happened to Ochopee?

Jeff Whichello

ISBN: 0615926029
ISBN 13: 9780615926025
Library of Congress Control Number: 2013921651
JFLU Publishing, Brandon, FL

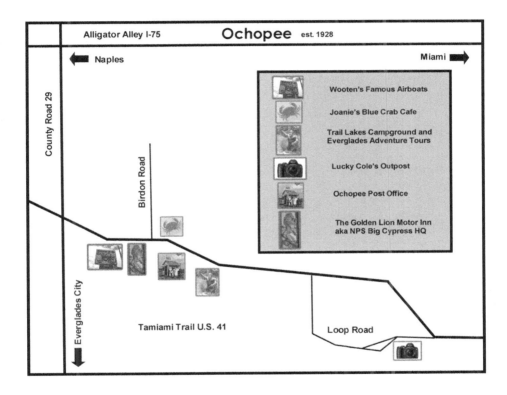

Alligator Alley I-75 **Ochopee** est. 1928

◀ Naples   Miami ▶

County Road 29

Birdon Road

Everglades City

Wooten's Famous Airboats

Joanie's Blue Crab Cafe

Trail Lakes Campground and
Everglades Adventure Tours

Lucky Cole's Outpost

Ochopee Post Office

The Golden Lion Motor Inn
aka NPS Big Cypress HQ

Tamiami Trail U.S. 41

Loop Road

CONTENTS

Part Four Simple Life

Part Five Casualties

Part Six   Mop Up

Balance

All aspects of life require balance: sacrifice with reward, regulation with independence, environmentalism with development. Too much reward without sacrifice spoils; too much regulation without independence enslaves; and too much environmentalism without development imprisons. To disregard the constitution and ruin the economic lives of the citizens it protects, for the sake of greed and political influence, should be illegal. To protect nature by eliminating humanity is immoral.

> Most people who settled the areas of Chokoloskee, Everglades, Ochopee, and the whole area were people who were really nonconformists. They wanted to live their own lives. They didn't want anyone to tell them what to do. They wanted to create their own world. -James Gaunt

> I think all the children look back on Ochopee as a good place to have been raised. It was a good life. We were all happy. -Daisy Gaunt

People First

JEANIE'S POEM

An Ohio farmer sought his fortune
In a swamp ridden with danger;
Fellow pioneers, Gaunt and Brown,
Soon felt him no longer a stranger.

Ken toiled and labored in muck on rainy days,
Pushed the water with pumps and pipes,
Worked the soil with sweat and blood,
Brought red, swollen fruit to life.

He gave no mind to creatures,
With their occasional passing through,
In early Ochopee they kept working,
Both he and his native crew.

At sundown, he slept in a trailer,
Perched on a spot of limestone,
With no companion to share his success,
His eyes closed to sleep-alone.

An Ohio housewife sought to escape,
The abuses of her spouse;
He beat her with his fist
And kept her in the house.

He railed her with his scorn,
Confusing love and pain,
Stripped her of her will,
Until her heart felt only shame.

A traitor to liberty,
Behind his face, intentions cruel,
A breaker of trust,
His desires; he made the rule.

She tried to find reason,
Pleading and begging alone,
In the end, he was no friend
And threw her out of her home.

On a visit to his origin,
Ken found Jeanie in a mess.
He paused to listen to the story
Of her recent homelessness.
Sparking like a worn lamp cord,
Once well-oiled, now a jumble of rust,
She sputtered and cried and hurt inside;
He pondered how to gain her trust.

With holding hands, he met her eye;
Her heart, he felt, had been weakened,
"Cheer up my dear, no longer fear;
You are only bruised-not beaten."

"I have a place; you would love it.
There you can be free in the wild."
He thought of their matching character;
She lifted her head and smiled.

On condition he built her a house,
Jeanie took her second chance at life.
On the edge of a swamp, in his trailer,
She lived on-as his wife.

The landscape drew her gaze,
Into a canvas of green and brown,
Jagged mismatched shapes and
Golden saw grass from the ground.

Thin naked aliens with big bushy heads,
The trees curved to the left and right.
She looked for the end of the grass,
It went on and on from sight.

Ken did not lie: her house he built.
At night, she listened to insects drone.
She began to learn who she used to be;
Her eyes closed to sleep at home.

The two shared a handful of years
Until the takers came,
Wielding agendas to erase humanity,
Labeling the people as the blame.

A traitor to liberty,
Behind their faces, intentions cruel,
A breaker of trust,
Their desires; they made the rule.

The family tried to find reason,
Pleading and begging alone.

In the end, the government was no friend
And threw them out of their home.

Ken never forgot-
Bitter until his death;
Jeanie loved him for all their years
And honored his final request.

She returned to the house,
Sat on the dock Ken built nearby,
Placed his ashes in the water,
Wiped her tears, and said, *"Good-bye."*

She visited the swamp year after year,
To sit on the dock by that place,
And talked to Ken about how she'd been;
In her mind, she could still see his face.

At age eighty-three, a stroke put her down,
Weakened in sight and speech.
She limped that year to the dock;
Its appearance, like her, worn and beat.

Something new, signs, she read: "No-trespass."
A man approached her and her fishing pole.
"You must leave; you cannot stay;
Now get out-you have to go."

"I lived here; we farmed and built our house.
Why don't you leave an old woman in peace?"
He dictated policy and regulation
Then threatened with police.

She never forgot-
Bitter until her death-
A friend, her caretaker in that last year,
Honored her final request.

Behind their house, across the swamp,
Ken and Jeanie live to this day.
Together in everlasting peace,
Now no one can take their home away.

SOMETHING FROM NOTHING

Ochopee, a place long before its naming, contained no marshes, highlands, palm trees, orchids, manatees, panthers, alligators, birds, Native Americans, politicians, or environmentalists. Sunk beneath an ocean, it waited. Time passed. Water receded; limestone emerged; and the seeds from plants and trees arrived by the wind and water. More time passed. Prehistoric tiny horses, sluggish sloths, massive cats, and wild mammoths walked through the land. Though these inhabitants vanished into extinction, new life never stopped coming to the peninsula. Animals and vegetation provided nourishment to sustain the first humans. They reached the area long after crossing a land bridge that connected Asia to Alaska. In time, additional settlers sailed their ships from Europe, and brought horses and boars from Spain and fruit, like the orange, from Southeast Asia.

Earth put the land up for use, and then humans, animals, and plants took advantage of the gift. In the last century, men armed with the modern age, stepped into South Florida. The once-underwater sand pit transformed again through the realization of hidden value in the soggy mud. To reach it, they made a road.

In 1918, forty-three miles of a man-made path started in Miami and cut west through the Everglades. James Franklin Jaudon, from Texas, financed the project, but when his Chevelier Corporation ran short of funds, Barron Gift Collier (from Tennessee) picked up the baton. He pushed on from the west and met Jaudon in the middle. In 1928, it was 283 miles long, and the access lay complete from Tampa to Miami: the Tamiami Trail, US 41. People came down the road. Some wanted to study the diversity of nature, but others desired to tap into the natural resources. Jaudon owned a great deal of land in Collier County, so he wished to sell some of it for development.

Edgar C. Gaunt, a descendant from a long line of Quakers, bought 250 acres of land from Jaudon at one hundred dollars each. With army tents and mosquito nets, he set up camp with the help of his twenty-eight-year-old son, James Gaunt. He hired men to help build a workers' quarters on pilings above the flood-prone pasture. They cleared a portion by using mules pulling mowers with sickle blades, and in October, the first crop of tomatoes went into the ground.

The development grew through the seasons to having several hundred people in three settlements, which included twenty-five Seminole natives living in their leaf-thatched dwellings and two other groups one white and one black both of which lived in the boarding houses provided by Gaunt.

Collier finished a railroad from Immokalee south through Everglades City, allowing for the movement of supplies into the small village. By 1932, it boasted a packing plant, boarding houses, a restaurant, a garage, a bulk plant, and a general store with a post office. At first electric power flowed from two DC Koehler plants southwest of the garage but were replaced by a two cylinder Fairbanks Morse diesel and a six cylinder standby International diesel. The water supply came from a wooden tank filled by an electric pump about 150 feet from James Gaunt's house.

One day, a Seminole native boy named Charley Tommy happened to be in the store, when a customer asked James for the name of the community surrounding him. James asked Charley what he called a big field or a farm in his language.

"O-cho-pe," said the boy. Soon after, the word *Ochopee* appeared on the official Florida map, pronounced, "O-cha-pee" by non-natives.

9

WEIMER

Carrying more than one man's share around his midsection and short on height, Ken Weimer appeared unremarkable. Some people thought he drank too much, while others questioned his embellished stories. In truth, Ken worked hard and played hard. He possessed secret powers in his hands-on skills for mechanics, expertise in instincts, natural strength of will, and a compassion for people. As an Ohio farmer, he worked on the land every day. The money generated from his crops funded sight-seeing trips to other parts of the country. When he stumbled upon the triumph of Ochopee with its new road, and nearby train he knew that he had found his next great adventure.

He returned home to save money, and in the late 1940s, he met with Franklin Jaudon and a salesman named Bird, from Miami. Jaudon and Bird created a farm a mile and a half west of Ochopee and called it *Birdon* the combination of their names. After purchasing four hundred acres of farmland adjacent to the development, Ken followed their lead and grew tomatoes. Miccosukee natives living in the area signed on to help.

Growing tomatoes taught Ken the skills of water manipulation. By the mid-1950s, new projects in town required water. He took money from the farming and invested it in the creation of Ochopee Water Company. He then built wellheads and laid miles of pipes. New power lines along the railroad allowed him to operate generators to run powerful pumps. In time, the new general store and an airboat and swamp-buggy operation paid Ken for his services. Around 1960, businessman Forrest Harmon helped Ken improve the water facility. Though tomato sales fell to an all-time low, real estate boomed for uses other than farming, so Ken pursued the logical next step and began a land-sale company. He erected a building to house the office along the border of Tamiami

Trail. Behind the office, he apportioned acreage for a planned community and named it Everglade Shores. To the average passerby, the blip of sparse grasses and coarse rocks where alligators, snakes, and scorpions roamed seemed like an uninhabitable wasteland. To Ken, the place represented an outdoorsman's paradise. He drew up his plan on paper, showing roads and plots for homes with water access.

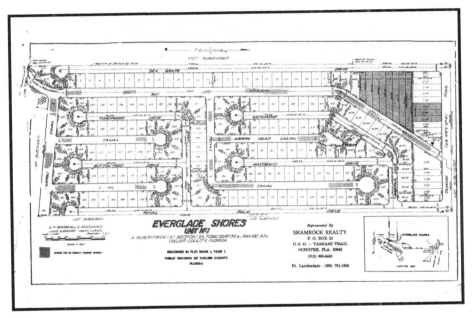

Ken Weimer's proposed community, 210 lots on eighty-three acres

Ken called on the help of his now business partner and friend, Forrest Harmon. Harmon's Ochopee Rock Company provided him the necessary stone to fill in the parts of the swamp required for home foundations and the expertise of demolition to create canals used for fishing. Harmon Rock employed experts in dynamite use, so Ken went to the literal task of blasting his idea into the swamp.

Google maps satellite image of Ken Weimer's development showing the manmade canals created by dynamite

Ken took orders for buyers for lots in his subdivision, including from Harmon. In the late sixties, he sold a neighboring plot of land along the Tamiami Trail to a family that was interested in building a motel. Though the idea seemed noble, Ken told the newcomer, "You're crazy to build a motel out here."

With the start of the 1970s, Ken Weimer lived day to day in a trailer at the back edge of Everglade Shores. He shared the land with a handful of homes-a fraction of its planned capacity. Ken felt the burden of loneliness. On a trip back to Ohio in 1971, he met a woman named Jeanie.

Jeanie had married young and had spent years under the violent physical, emotional, and mental abuses of her first husband, which eventually led to the meltdown of the marriage. Then in her late thirties, after years of heavy drinking and a life of self-neglect, she met Ken. They married in 1972, and he convinced her to come with him to the trailer in the middle of the Everglades. She agreed-only if he promised to build them a real house someday. Months after being in the trailer with Jeanie, Ken realized that an efficiency apartment in the motel at the front of his property seemed like a more reasonable plan. For a year and a half they lived at Ochopee's Golden Lion Motor Inn, room 124.

Ken constructed their house on the farthest corner of his development, overlooking a canal, where native friends built them a leaf-thatched dwelling in the backyard. Elated, Jeanie sat on a brand-new dock and spent evenings catching her dinner, while Ken visited with some of the Ochopee business leaders at the home of the general store owner, Frances Watson.

Every Friday night, into the early morning, these residents played poker with an ante of twenty-five cents. The wilderness secluded them from civilization and provided blue crabs from the streams, which Frances boiled until they turned red. They sat around the table, socializing and toasting-a celebration of friendship and humanity.

WOOTEN

Labelle, a small South Florida town, surrounded Raymond Wooten as a child in the 1920s. A strong and tall boy, he left behind his formal education of just eight years to work the fields of Arcadia. At age seventeen, he found his wife, Lillian, age sixteen, and so they began the business of raising a family. Richard, Willard, and Gene arrived in the world.

Early automobiles required constant maintenance, and Raymond discovered his knack for fixing them. By expanding his skill set from farming to mechanics, he qualified for higher-paying work. His brother then convinced him to move his family to a small swamp community sixty miles south of Labelle, where a service station in Ochopee needed a mechanic. After settling into the new location, he found time to take on additional employment with the Humble Oil Corporation. Finding oil in Collier County became the primary company mission. In 1943, with Raymond's help, oil breached the earth. The state of Florida gave the company a monetary award for the discovery, and Raymond continued to witness the government's interest in Florida oil.

Because of the scarcity of roads in the Everglades, Raymond used a propless, flat-bottom boat with a giant fan blade attached to a car engine to cross the marsh. One afternoon, he and his son Richard tried out a boat they used for catching frogs. Tourists spotted them parked in the water near a bank. Intrigued by the contraption, having never seen such a thing, they offered some money for the simple return of a ride. After the trip, an idea came to Raymond. He took on work from a variety of sources, including the garage, the Oil Company, and farming. When he saved enough money, he approached a hunter friend named Speck Coker and purchased two-and-a-half acres of land in Ochopee. He then hired workers to help raise a structure to store sheets of aluminum and tools. In the canal that fed water to his property, he ignored any possibility of an unseen creature and stepped into the muddy water. Laboring many days, he used his bare hands to dig out an area for boats to launch. He pounded with hammers, molded metal, and popped rivets, until his first commercial boat came into being. Some vessels that he made held five people and some twenty with lengths of twelve feet and greater. He retrofitted 500 and 550 horsepower Cadillac engines with metal fan blades as tall as a man and secured them to the back of the floating contraptions. He then met Ken Weimer and paid him to provide his land with fresh water for the family and his business. In 1953, the official Wooten's Airboats opened to the public, providing an experience like no other before and no other since. A roller coaster without rails, Wooten's hovering crafts let people ride the swamp, seeing its beauty from a bird's eyes. It took them to unknown and unreachable places. Raymond shared his love of nature and the wild with all of his visitors, and in turn, they allowed him to expand his vision.

He discovered dry seasons: a time in the swamp, just before the summer, when the water level dropped, and so running boats became a difficult chore. To keep the business open, he busted rocks by hand and dug deep into the mud. He installed Artesian wells to help pull up the desired flow.

While family members increased in number, workers did also, and the family business flourished among satisfied customers bent on telling their friends of the incredible ride. After purchasing four hundred acres, Raymond tried to incorporate a marina, but the government refused to give him a permit.

Forrest Harmon assisted Raymond in the use of dynamite, a product made from pine trees in Immokalee to the north of Ochopee. Harmon Rock Company blasted the launching area and used draglines to make room for additional airboats. By 1972, Raymond's sweat and blood covered every inch of the property. People from all over the world experienced Wooten's tour of the river of grass. He invested over a million dollars each year in advertisement so that his billboards appeared all along the Tamiami Trail, and into Naples. His television commercials broadcast across central and north Florida. From a meager existence of picking oranges to latching onto a single idea and pursuing his relentless work ethic, Raymond Wooten followed through to see his life's work complete.

SHEALY

Jack Shealy's ancestors lived in remote places throughout the Everglades in the 1800s. By the early 1900s, his family found their way to Coconut Grove, south of Miami. He spent his childhood discovering the ocean in fishing boats. During trips to neighboring wetlands, he hunted wild game with his father, and learned techniques passed down for generations. They built traps for boars, sloshed through the night mud for frogs, and shot turkeys. The farther Jack travelled and the more time he spent in the wilderness, the more he realized where he belonged.

As a young married man, he traveled a hundred miles inland and came across the small, but hopeful, community of Ochopee. A real estate purveyor named Ken Weimer offered Jack and Evelyn an assortment of properties. They decided on one and settled the land. By 1963, the Shealys added to the family their second son, David, while toddler Jack, Jr. spent days watching his parents build a permanent home. At an early age, Jack Jr. learned from his father about the dangers of the wild territory as panthers, black bears, water moccasins, and alligators made brief appearances. Educated on plant and animal life, weather and terrain, the Shealy brothers took lessons from their parents but just as often from Mother Nature. In 1970, Evelyn filled the position of postmaster after the retirement of pioneer Sidney Brown. Most newcomers to the community did business with Evelyn, and they soon became aware of her husband's new endeavor, Trail Lakes campground. Jack Sr. cleared places for motor homes, trailers, and tents around an assortment of scenic ponds. He built a bathhouse with hot and cold running water and then installed a laundry facility. Some hunters came for a season; others stayed year-round. They bought supplies from a small store that Jack assembled at the front of his acreage, facing the Tamiami Trail. Shealy offered the nature-seeking world his passion and knowledge of a place many considered a hazard.

At ten-years-old, David sighted something strange. An ape-like creature walked on two legs and stood much taller than his father as it crossed a field and vanished into the sawgrass. Stories about such a beast lingered in his mind, put there by talk around campfires. This animal-man that emitted a foul odor thought to be caused by its hiding in alligator dens-appeared to a rare few.

In 1976, teenagers Jack Jr. and David walked after their parents into the first Skunk-Ape festival. Bill Mitchell, a local hunter, claimed that he saw the legend and wanted everyone to know, so he arranged an elaborate event at a special place in Ochopee. Known as Oasis, a small airport contained a two-story building adorned with a Lockheed Constellation airliner on stilts. David watched a man who wore a dark, fuzzy monkey suit jumping up and down and waving his arms from the roof of the structure. While bluegrass music spilled around a giant Ferris wheel, visitors hoped to win the raffle drawings, and children took turns climbing a long steel pole coated with grease for the winning of a prize. Mitchell talked with Jack Sr. about adding a restaurant at the facility and a lounge inside of the aircraft. Ochopee Motel owner, Daniel Whichello, listened, while his wife and two children waited for local pilot, Harold Enquist, (aka Happy Harry) to take them on a ride in his small plane parked on the runway. Next to them, Forrest Harmon handed ten dollars to another pilot and helped Jack Jr. into a helicopter for his personal ascent.

Oasis

THE SMALLEST POST OFFICE

Since 1932, Ochopee's bustling post office provided all of the necessary communications for the village, but in the early 50s, it met its demise. That morning, before the birds awoke, a transient man passed into sleep and left his lit cigarette burning. He never woke again as flames destroyed him and the boarding house where he slept. Next went the store and the post office. With the loss of the store went important paperwork showing who owed and who paid, and without the post office, mail flow ceased. Some residents moved away, while others stayed to rebuild, but with no store to provide supplies, life fell into a primitive existence.

Post Master Sidney Brown with the help of his son Ralph decided that the first thing they needed was to get the post office up and running. The next day they walked out to the tomato fields and dismounted a 7' x 8' shed used for storing insecticides from a car chassis. After dragging it back to the devastated scene, they cleaned it and went to work installing the devices of mail organization, shelves, bins, etc. Ochopee life continued.

HARMON

Part business man, part engineer, and at heart a pioneer, Forrest Harmon leant his lifelong experience to the government of the United States in the early 1940s. Scientists toiled in a fever to build the first atomic bomb to stop the Axis powers during the Second World War. He saw to their comfort and security in the housing that he helped design and build in The Manhattan Project.

In the 1950s, Forrest's love of travelling and outdoor sports fishing led him to Ochopee. The founding of Ochopee Rock Company gave the fire-devastated farming project an infusion of commerce. It turned out that the settlement possessed a treasure other than the farm land: rock. A vast quantity of Oolite-a type of stone used in building roads-could be found just about everywhere in the Everglades. Florida's booming road system required this component, and the South Florida rock surpassed government standards for quality, requiring little refinement. With farming to the side, the tiny town turned valuable once again, and so hundreds of people arrived to participate. Forrest managed four trailer parks to house newcomers. A big man, well over six feet tall, he often wore a white sailor hat with a black brim and a round top. He dressed in a sort of dinner jacket, where he kept a stash of tobacco for his bulbous pipe. People regarded his garbled southern inflection as difficult to understand, but over time they did, and then referred to him as "a sweet man, who would give the shirt off his back." He and his wife, Donna, bought a piece of property from Ken Weimer. Ken and Forrest became noteworthy business partners, friends, and then neighbors in Ken's development. Forrest liked to get things done, and with a bottomless reservoir of energy, he started additional projects. With Ken turning his attention to real estate, Forrest built an improved water company and assisted him with dynamite for making fishing canals.

In the mid-70s, Midge Lessor traveled from Miami to Ochopee seeking a better life for her family. Around 1976 she met Forrest.

Forrest Harmon, by Midge Lessor

> *Forrest was a fine Kentucky gentleman and a smart business man. He is one of the few who fought the government many times. He and his wife Donna were so kind and were pillars of the community.*
>
> *I was very sad and down-hearted when I went to the Golden Lion one night. It must have reflected on my face. He walked up to me and said, "what's wrong with you honey, you look like you just lost your best friend?" That's when I told him it was worse than that. I told him that I might lose my property because I had invested in an old diesel dump truck so I could make more than three dollars an hour pounding crab traps night and day. He said, "Let's have a drink and talk this over." I explained that I expected an off-the-road job and was turned down because I was a woman. I had all of the money saved for the property payment and no job. To my surprise, He said, "You want a job honey? Have your truck at my rock pit in Ochopee in the morning." With his kindness, he saved my property! I am forever indebted to Forrest and the Golden Lion. If you had a problem or something to sell or barter for, you would go to the Golden Lion-our meeting place. Someone would come up with a solution.*

Forrest Harmon (back) and Mant Spaulding (front)

WATSON

Frances arrived in Everglades City in 1949. She looked for the adventure of making her own way, the same as all pioneer families. Stout, quick witted, and capable, she possessed a sharp charisma. No fear stopped Frances from telling people how she felt about them. Hard work brought out her best, and after spending time on the island of Everglades City, she brought her family to Ochopee. No stranger to hammering nails and lifting lumber, in 1956, she helped her husband build their house. When he passed away, she remarried in 1958 to a man named Joe Watson.

Walter and Flo Heirs arrived in Ochopee in 1937 and farmed tomatoes. Years later they ran a store. Walter estimated 75 percent of the natives bought from it, and so the family developed a close friendship with them. In 1959, the store burned, but they rebuilt a larger, modern facility, which Frances and Joe purchased in 1960 and renamed it *Ma Watson's General Store*. With Frances at the helm of the Ochopee grocery, it took on quite a different character. She stood behind the counter all through the day, ringing in customer orders, and speaking with them. Some described her as a sort of carnie-like individual, with a rugged way about her, though she helped the poor when they needed food and clothing. For those who needed insulting, she obliged them as well. Her reputation (as a person who handed out insults to those who toyed with her or did not quite look at her right) traveled. One of the family members, Joe Kerrick, saw to capitalize on the swamp woman's personality and designed a shirt to sell in the store.

A pattern from a shirt sold at the Watson Store

An experienced hunter explains the custom:

> Cutting the shirt tail off when a hunter, especially a young rookie, misses a deer is just an old tradition. I've missed deer through the years, and friends suggested my shirt-tail be cut-in a joking manner. But it never was, probably due to those ribbing me having also missed deer at one time or another. What I say here is not to say that some folks do not honor the tradition fervently as a tool to train young hunters to take more careful aim so as not to wound or cripple animals, causing unjustifiable suffering. Yep, I would guess that training hunters might be what started the tradition.

The general store created memories: such as the giant jar of *Red Smith's* pickled sausages sitting on the counter or the rack of multi-colored Seminole jackets for sale. A necessary oasis, it offered beer, wine, Thunder Bird, Mad Dog, meats, lard, soap, clothes, blankets, animal feed, and fishing and hunting licenses. Goods sprawled across the rows of wooden shelves in the one-room store. People remember most of all the customer service of Sam. Even with Frances away in a back room, patrons who came through the front door, were greeted with the infamous, high-pitched, "Hello," that seemed to come from nowhere.

"Hello?"

"Hello."

"Hello?"

"Hello."

The echo ceased when the person looked up to see a large bird cage containing a small black myna bird.

Frances enjoyed gambling and attending horse races, yet she did not drink much. Her real passion was people, as she made her home a place of welcome for everyone. Late Friday nights, friends in the community visited for cards, drink, food, and conversation. In this manner, she gained a full life in Ochopee.

WHICHELLO

Larger and stronger than the other children his age, twelve-year-old Harlan Whichello worked the Pennsylvania summers on a farm to help feed his impoverished family. Times of the depression wreaked havoc on many Americans, but with six kids to feed and their son Bill in the hospital with tuberculosis, Harlan's parents had little choice but to send him to a farm.

For two summers, Harlan worked caring for turkeys until his family moved to Hamtramck, Michigan in 1929. With just an eighth-grade education, he managed to score well on all of the entrance exams for the Henry Ford Trade School. Because Ford provided free tuition, books, and a savings account for orphan children and the poor, Harlan had a chance. At age fourteen, he walked with his oldest brother, Richard, to school down Eight Mile Road, and entered the auto-manufacturing plant to start his first day of an apprenticeship. In two years, he accepted a full-time position specializing in electricity and worked in the electrical department at Ford's manufacturing plant.

Harlan met his wife, Pauline-both teenagers-and they started a family. Their first child died at age one. Their next child reached one-years-old and died as well. Their third child came to the world still-born. To cope with the grief and strain on the marriage, Harlan devoted his time to work. Around 1940, he left Ford and joined his two brothers to start their own business: Walton Die and Mold. They spent weeks searching around the backs and sides of manufacturing companies, finding an assortment of old scrap metal. Rummaging through junk-yards, they picked up worn-out machines that were rusting in the open air. Devices cast out as waste became, to the brothers, buried treasure: surface grinders, bridge port mills, metal laves, band saws, welders, punch presses, dies, molds, and even old heaters-all of which they assembled in their new shop.

They toiled for weeks, working sixteen-hour days repairing, cleaning, polishing the equipment, and building wooden work-benches and other furniture. When they finally opened, they could only afford to run the shop for one shift per day. Months into operation, Pauline found out that she carried a fourth child, Daniel. In the next five years, their business prospered, and with the war effort in need, they tripled production, making parts for the military. Pauline continued to have children that survived.

February 10, 1947. The allies signed peace treaties with the minor European Axis countries, while back in the United States, the government looked to collect profits from companies that made contracts with the military. Congress assigned a panel of judges to hear cases of those businesses unable to pay the amounts calculated by government accountants in the required time frames. Walton's owners received notices from the government to give them every penny owed in ninety days. The government came to Harlan and his brothers for help, and now, in the faces of the uncaring messengers, Harlan felt betrayed. Rather than face imprisonment on profiteering charges, Richard and Harlan dismantled the factories and sold the machines and the buildings, one by one, to pay the fees. Harlan was bankrupted. Cursing in anger, he vowed to never work with the government again. He sat in his house with a pregnant wife, three little boys, and the threat of not being able to feed them.

> While Richard handled the remnants of Walton, Bill begged for help for his self-started, custom-trailer-hitch business in his garage. The venture became unmanageable, so he and Harlan went looking for a place to lease a building in Belleville, Michigan. Draw-tite grew fast, and in the years to come, it made the family millions and created thousands of jobs for the economy, but then the government came again to take from Harlan his successes. The National Park Service in Michigan's Upper Peninsula used eminent domain to take property for the purpose of widening a nature-bound, rustic road. Officials required the improved road for use by their convoys of trucks that roared back and forth through the once-quiet woods. They then took other properties, adding to an enormous park across the north of Michigan.

Harlan hunted big game and fished across Canada, Alaska, and Michigan before visiting Florida around 1960. In the comfortable climate he embarked on extensive fishing excursions. He met a man who owned a real estate office in Ochopee. Ken Weimer's development, Everglade Shores seemed the perfect place for a possible retirement location. So Harlan and Pauline built a house in Ken's community.

In the mid-1960s, the board of Draw-tite arrived at a decision to sell the company. Against Harlan's will, he found himself fifty-two-years-old and retired. Having a life-long pension and a savings, he called his children-ages twenty-five to fourteen: Daniel, Edward, John, Nancy, Patty, and Kathy-around the dinner table one evening. He offered them their inheritance money-early-for an investment of their choosing. The eldest, Daniel, wanted to start a small mom-and-pop motel with his new wife, Marge. When his siblings decided to participate, the plan evolved into a larger motel, and then they added a restaurant and a bar. Ochopee's motel opened two days before Christmas, 1970.

The Golden Lion Motor Inn, 1970

Harlan Whichello in Ochopee

1969
Harlan and Daniel Whichello with Jack Barrett

TIME LINE

1928	The Tamiami Trail, aka US 41, opened, linking Tampa and Miami, built by Jaudon and Collier
1929	Edgar and James Gaunt began pre-Ochopee
1932	Ochopee named and a post office opened
Early 1940s	Ken Weimer bought land in Ochopee from Jaudon, Raymond Wooten bought land in Ochopee from Speck Coker and Jack Shealy, Sr. bought land from Ken Weimer
1943	Raymond witnessed oil found in the swamp
1949	Frances arrived in Everglades City
1953	Wooten's Airboats opened and Ochopee burned-the smallest post office opened
Mid	Forrest Harmon's Ochopee Rock Company started 1950s
1960	Joe and Frances Watson purchased the Ochopee store and Ma Watson's General Store opened

1970   Evelyn Shealy became postmaster and The Golden Lion Motor Inn opened

1976   First Skunk Ape Festival

Takers

CONFLICT OF INTEREST

January 1969. California native Richard M. Nixon lifted his hand and swore before the country:

> And will to the best of my ability, preserve, protect, and defend
> the constitution of the United States, so help me God.

He then became the president of the United States of America. Months later, he and his federal transportation staff affirmed the need for a project, already in progress, forty-five miles west of Miami. In the wake of the age of jumbo jets, the Dade County Port Authority accepted an initial $500,000 from the Federal Aviation Administration to build six runways on thirty-five square miles of acreage. The project began in 1968 when a bulldozer cut through the dirt in front of Florida governor Claude Kirk, another Californian, who made his approval known. Many of the airlines did not consider a new remote jetport in the middle of the Everglades useful, and those concerned for the environment believed the intrusion on nature to be a tragedy for the wildlife. Others speculated that plans existed for an industrial park following the venture, which aimed to boost sales for Collier County land and thus increase profits.

From New York, Nathaniel P. Reed moved to Jupiter Island, Florida to help his parents develop their hotel and real estate business. The Reeds dedicated land to concrete and steel structures, but they developed with nature in mind. When Kirk ran for governor, Reed assisted him in the win. The governor returned the favor by appointing Reed as his environmental advisor, which gave him a pollution-control commission to oversee. In the midst of his duties, Reed met Joe B. Browder. Browder, born in Texas, first moved to Florida at age three, and then returned to

Texas at age thirteen. With Florida on his mind, he made his way back after turning twenty-two. In 1961, he became a member of the Audubon Society, and years later, his limited participation in stopping the construction of a Florida oil refinery contributed to his desire to protect Florida's natural environments. He left a career in 1968 as a Miami television producer to pursue Miami development politics, which led him to Reed.

Most people considered the Miami jetport a done deal in the summer of 1969. Construction was due to complete in a year. Browder educated Reed on the enterprise and expressed his immense dissatisfaction. Browder gained Reed's trust and friendship and then invited him on a plane ride over the construction site. Upon seeing bulldozers clearing away the trees and foliage, Reed thought of what Browder had said about saving the environment. Convinced of his words, he approached Governor Kirk, a person not so concerned about environmental matters, but he did possess an interest in aiding the underdog against dominant adversaries. After hearing his friend's request, he took up the cause presented.

Arthur R. Marshall, born in South Carolina, worked as a biologist for the Florida Fish and Wildlife Commission. He received a call from Reed requesting assistance with a plan to try to stop the jetport from being finished. Marshall and Browder assembled a list of 119 questions concerning the impact of fuel spills and air and noise pollution on birds. Governor Kirk then called a meeting in Miami with the Dade County Port Authority. Environmental advisor Reed, biologist Marshall, and governor Kirk represented Browder's primary team. They sat together at a restaurant, facing a group they opposed: Port Authority director, planner, and builder Alan Stewart; Miami mayor, Steve Clark; Mayor Chuck Hall; deputy director of the port authority, Richard Judy; and others. The jetport builders looked upon the intervention with some confusion as to the agenda. Marshall and Kirk presented their series of questions to them, but they were met with a sense of dismissal. The jetport-backed, funded, and in full steam of being created-was already a reality to the creators. They did not come to the gathering prepared to answer a bombardment of questions or face hostility. During the event, Robert W. Padrick, who at one time headed the Central and South Florida Flood Control District, spoke:

> If we approach the problem reasonably and spend the money to
> solve it, surely, if we can land men on the moon, we can land air-
> planes without hurting anything.

The meeting did little to attain successful communication between sides.
Stewart believed the attack to be an exaggeration of emotion for political gain. The
mayor responded to the perceived negativity with hostile words of his own and left
with a feeling of being invaded. Browder's group left more determined to defeat the
jetport.

Browder mobilized an army of people from the Sierra Club, the Audubon
Society, the National Parks Association, and some authors. He used connections
with media to gain support for the cause through national magazines and news-
papers. Readers who had never stepped foot in Florida and who had no knowledge
of the state or its people became interested, and they donated money. On the local
front, Reed convinced Kirk (up for reelection at the end of the year) to pull his support for the jetport project.

"A vote for birds and alligators right now is going to be politically rewarding,"
Reed told him. Kirk went to talk to Walter Hickel, a former Alaskan governor and
developer. Hickel wished to improve his less-than-perfect environmental record, so
he allowed himself to be appointed to Nixon's cabinet as Secretary of the Interior.
When Kirk talked with Hickel about the jetport project and its possible relocation
out of Dade County, Hickel realized an opportunity. He thought that if he joined
the fight, this act might somehow help correct his political past. Hickel then toured
the jetport site, which by the end of the summer contained one, two-mile-long
runway and a control tower with thirteen million tax-payer dollars invested. Kirk
and Hickel camped out a few evenings in the swamp, enjoying the outdoors and
discussing the jetport over drinks. By the end of the trip, Hickel agreed to make
the Everglades his number-one issue. He then spoke with the transportation secretary, John Volpe. They came to the conclusion that cutting federal funds from the
project would stop it. Hickel took the idea to Nixon, and to help convince him, he
mentioned Senator Henry Jackson. Jackson, from Washington State, made plans
to run for the presidency of the United States. He caught wind of the battle forming against the Miami airport, and with his own group of supporters, organized a

hearing in Miami. Hickel presented Nixon with the situation of Jackson, a democratic challenger. The idea of taking the political reigns away from Jackson on the environmental issue of the jetport seemed to please Nixon. He ordered a study for Hickel's Department of the Interior to be coordinated by biologist Arthur Marshall.

September 1969. The results showed that the aviation plan would destroy the entire Everglades. A study finished by the National Academies of Science and Engineering showed that many of the problems created by the development could be minimized if the area surrounding it was left in its natural state and access to its connecting transportation corridors limited. A third study by the Overview Corporation, a firm headed by the previous Secretary of the Interior, Levi Stewart Udall from Arizona, was completed. After review of the evidence, deputy director of the port authority, Richard Judy, said that there would be no fear because land from another proposed location could be sold. The money would then be used to buy up all of the land around the jetport in order to make sure it remained safe. With no intention of listening to any of the studies other than the one he ordered, Nixon commanded that the project be stopped. The following year, it opened as a training facility with one runway.

January, 1970. Reubin O' Donovan Askew from Oklahoma was sworn in as governor of Florida, having defeated Claude Kirk, once told by Nathaniel Reed that a vote for birds would become a political reward.

BIG CYPRESS SWAMP

In the past, Joe Browder worked as a bag boy, stocker, delivery driver, radio news reporter, disc jockey, police officer, television news reporter, producer, and, in the late sixties, an environmentalist. He gained experience and made friendships by his efforts to help defeat an oil refinery, and a jetport as well as from making visits to Washington, DC, to find support for the protection of Biscayne Bay and the Everglades. In 1969, a friend invited him to join a new organization called Friends of the Earth. At the start of the next year, he finished up his duties at the Audubon Society and moved to Washington to become Conservation Director. His new tasks involved helping the group set up their national conservation strategy.

The jetport and Miami sat to the north of the Everglades National Park, already under government control, but in the same vicinity, a swamp later given the name, Big Cypress, remained in the hands of private citizens. Even before the jetport, Browder and others considered the notion of a plan to protect this area by letting government control it.

Lawton Mainor Chiles, Jr., from Florida, a member of the House of Representatives, ran for senator in 1970. People dubbed him, "Walking Lawton," because he walked from one end of Florida to the other end-over one thousand miles. Browder helped draft a bill, and he and Chiles looked for help from a retired senator named Holland. Browder went along with Chiles to talk with Holland. Throughout 1970, Holland met with his friends in the senate and other areas of government about supporting the bill. In February, he cosponsored legislation with fellow congressman Edward John Gurney (from Maine) to buy the swamp, but the bill did not get enough votes to pass. Browder's friend Nathaniel Reed received a promotion to Assistant Interior Secretary of the United States, and together with the secretary, they presented the White House and Nixon with a US geological survey

defining the proposed land. While being kept informed about environmental protection projects-such as the creation of national parks-Nixon's hands overflowed
with challenges: such as the Vietnam War, the economy, and an energy crisis. The
ever-increasing dependency and use of foreign oil reserves played a part to influence
government's search for additional sources inside of the country. Previous discovery
of oil in the cypress swamp made it a possible target.

Henry Jackson, senate committee chairman on interior and insular affairs, initiated his campaign to run for president, and though he was not able to capitalize on
the jetport project, he saw opportunity with Big Cypress. He planned to kick off his
presidential campaign by calling a hearing in Miami to reveal his bill. As with the
jetport, word reached Nixon, and to reduce a possible challenger to the presidency,
he acted with haste and told his domestic advisor, John Ehrlichman, to go after
the Big Cypress. The advisor called Reed and informed him of the decision. Once
educated on the plan, the governor of Florida, Reubin Askew, agreed. Nixon then
appointed Reed as Secretary of the Interior for Fish, Wildlife, and National Parks.

November 24, 1971. President Richard M. Nixon addressed the public in a
speech, a few days before Jackson's hearing. He proclaimed to the world that the US
government would carry out a plan to take half-a-million acres of Florida land. He
read estimates from the study. The taxpayers would pay $150 million dollars, and
twenty-one thousand landowners would lose their land.

In Ochopee, located in the area to be taken, people felt disbelief and betrayal
from what they perceived as an attack on liberty, freedoms, and the constitution.

MIAMI HEARING

On the morning of Jackson's hearing, landowners and business leaders from Ochopee gathered in the restaurant of the Golden Lion Motor Inn. Harlan Whichello, son Daniel, his accountant John Soldavini, Ken Weimer, and Forrest Harmon sat drinking coffee and discussing Nixon's speech. The lobby filled with citizens preparing to attend the event. Three women dressed in Native American attire came through the front doors. Many knew them well as chiefs of a local Seminole tribe. One of them said to Daniel, "We heard about the meeting for the land from Mrs. Watson. Can we go with you?"

Harlan and Daniel drove the women the eighty miles to Miami. A packed Miami Dade College auditorium filled with conversation from the first floor and balcony. A few people held tall white signs that read: *Federal Land Grab*. Senator Jackson and Senator Chiles sat at desks on a stage, where Jackson beat a gavel and called into a microphone for quiet. The senators introduced themselves, and the crowd spilled forth a wave of boos. Jackson banged the gavel again and again. With order established, he spoke:

> My new legislation will protect the water needed for the Everglades
> National Park and southwest Florida cities; although, I regret that
> it will affect many landowners, who will be required to sell their
> land. I urge the speedy passing of this most important legislation.

Boos erupted from the crowd. Jackson informed everyone about previously submitted questions. He then began going through cards and called on individuals. Arthur Marshall, the ecologist from Miami, stood and took a microphone from an assistant who brought it to his seat.

The nearly untouched wilderness must be protected if South Florida is to have enough water for future needs. The central issue in this matter is water—water for the park, for plant life, for wildlife, for marine resources, and for recreation. The area must be preserved to provide an important refuge for the endangered animals.

Upon being called, one of his colleagues added:

The Big Cypress should be preserved because of its unique plants and animals as well as the water. They are virtually certain to disappear if the Big Cypress is diminished and destroyed by drainage and development.

Jay Landers, assistant to the governor, stood and spoke into a microphone: "I have a prepared statement from Governor Askew." Jay looked down at a paper and read:

By making this area a park, we have the opportunity to show man that he has learned the vulnerability of the natural environment.

Robert Shevin, state attorney general, took his turn and said:

I and my cabinet completely support this legislation and its speedy passing by Congress.

The crowd erupted again. Collier County manager, W. H. Turner, took his turn and said:

I wonder why this hearing wasn't held in Collier County instead of Dade County. The Big Cypress area should not be selected for a park site until a current three-year, three-million-dollar study of the Everglades is completed, or that money will have been wasted.

The crowd applauded, and he continued:

> This park is going to be a huge loss of revenue that will affect the
> county if the land is taken off their tax rolls. The land going into
> that park is one-third of the property in the county. The federal
> government each year should make up this tax loss to us, and
> property owners should be paid right away-not twenty or thirty
> years later.

The people than cheered, and a man raised a sign that read: "*In twelve years the government still has not paid for the land in Everglades National Park.*"

Jackson banged his gavel and yelled, "If you do not keep in order, you will be forced to leave the auditorium! This is an impartial hearing. We can't make up our minds just because you have cheering sections out there!"

The crowd quieted.

"The Big Cypress is jeopardized by the pressure for progress based on, sometimes, well-intended but, too often, ill-planned development," Senator Chiles countered Turner's statements.

Once the recorded questions were completed, Jackson called on anyone who raised their hand. The hearing went on for a few hours, with words from conservationists, government, landowners, business leaders, and even a former Florida governor, Fuller Warren, whose group argued that the government officials had been misinformed about the value of the water and the wildlife resources of the swamp. Miccosukee tribe chairman, Buffalo Tiger, looked for governmental assurances that the natives be guaranteed the right to operate restaurants and motels within the preserve. Landowners pointed out that water from the Big Cypress was only a small part of the flow into the Everglades Park, and they accused Jackson and Chiles of playing politics.

A man from Collier County rose up and spoke into the microphone: "The acquisition is not according to our US Constitution. This is not democracy."

Jackson interrupted him: "We're trying to bring government to the people. What other form of government would have a public hearing? I think this is a democracy."

"Well, it's not!" a member of the audience yelled. Several people applauded. Jackson banged on his gavel for silence.

Washington lobbyist, Browder, stood and spoke: "If this land is not acquired by the government, it will be bought and developed."

While the crowd slowed again to order, Jackson informed the people that he had another engagement and must be excused. He told them that Senator Lawton Chiles would continue to answer any questions. A whirl of anger fanned the room as Jackson left. A resident of Ochopee raised his hand and spoke to Lawton and said, "Those bird watchers are taking our land away. You walked a lot to get elected didn't you?"

"Yes sir. I did," Chiles answered.

"Well, I walked a lot too. I was in the infantry during the war, and I walked in Italy. I walked in Sicily. They finally shot me before the war was over. Now I'm on disability payments, and all I've got left in the world is ten acres of land in Big Cypress."

Much of the crowd shouted their approval, and then many wanted to speak, but Lawton was overwhelmed.

Sitting in the auditorium with his father and neighbors from Ochopee, Daniel overheard that a few men from town went to follow after Jackson. He later learned that Jackson led them to a location where he sat signing and selling his new book.

PREPARING FOR WAR

December 12, 1971. Over a hundred local landowners, concerned citizens, and family members met in the restaurant diner of the Golden Lion on a Friday night. They crammed in wherever they fit. Harlan and Daniel Whichello, as well as Ken Weimer, attended. Organizer of the meeting, Forrest Harmon, chairman of the East Collier County Land Owners' Improvement Committee, stood up at the side of the room.

"OK, I'm calling the meeting to order. There's going to be another public hearing in Naples early next year. We need to consider selecting a panel of people to take them our message."

"I think landowners should sign petitions," Said Ellis Chism of Miami, "and they should also show their backing for the jetport site."

"No, the jetport isn't important right now. We need to worry about our families," said an attendee.

"We can't do anything for the jetport," said another.

"Many of us were not able to speak at the last hearing," said a concerned resident, "and when W. H. Turner spoke, Jackson treated him very disrespectfully."

Ewell F. Moore, Collier County commissioner, spoke:

> I urge everyone to send letters and petitions to their congressmen and state representatives. Large groups have difficulties presenting their side of any question. Not everyone can be heard, but you can be heard if you write that letter to Senator Chiles and Senator Jackson and to any congressman involved, because this thing will definitely have to go through two houses to get approval.

An attendee then said, "Why do the government officials listen to bird watchers before they listen to us?"

Moore looked at him and said, "It's unfortunate that one of those bird watchers has the weight of about one hundred of us." He looked around the room. "Let's see if we can't get one hundred of us to every one of them!"

A. C. Hancock, a county commissioner, a well-established public servant, and defender of the rights of citizens in south Florida said, "They think they have the right to take our land and to kick us around!"

Once everyone settled into the meeting, they started the planning to determine options for saving their land.

"I think Raymond Wooten should be on the panel," said W. H. Turner, Collier County manager.

Raymond then spoke:

> They want to take our land because of the underlying oil and natural gas reserves in the Big Cypress. I personally helped with the well digging for the Sunniland area. The whole area is underlaid with oil and natural gas. People have been sent out from government to brainwash everyone about how the area should be saved for recreation and a watershed.

A. C. Hancock, by Glenda Hancock

> *A.C. was a self-accomplished man. He was serious about business but enjoyed a little party once in a while. He was dedicated to his service as County Commissioner and loved serving the people. One thing I remember about him in the early seventies is that he would take every call from anyone in his district that had a concern. We learned that when the phone rang, we were to continue on with dinner because he was going to take the time he needed to hear what the person on the other end had to say. He*

served as a county commissioner for twelve years. He lost to the gentleman from Marco-can't remember his name. It was quite a blow to A. C. He returned to running his marina and helping with the motel he and his wife had built in 1955. After a short time, he was approached by Aubrey Rogers and asked if he would work as a deputy. He told him if he could do the marine patrol from Chokoloskee, south and north to Marco, he would. He did this until 1986 when he retired.

A.C. was born on Sandfly Island in 1922. He graduated from Everglades City School and then went to the navy with his brother Dennis on the buddy plan. That is another story.

A.C. was a stern man when he spoke. He was not a man of many words, but when one of his grandbabies came into the room, he became a big fluffy bundle of love. When a new baby came along, he had to be the one to hold and love on them. All three of my kids remember his dippy, dippy do. This was his communication with them. They would laugh, and he would just bust out laughing.

DEVALUE

After the American Civil War, a period of government reconstruction resulted in the United States. Many felt that the governors of states possessed too much power. Creation of the Florida cabinet helped keep a balance. Its six elected members held an equal vote with the governor in executive decisions. The cabinet positions were:

- **Commissioner of Agriculture**
  Supervised all matters pertaining to agriculture

- **Commissioner of Education**
  Chief Officer of public education

- **Comptroller**
  The state's chief fiscal officer

- **Secretary of State**
  Maintained the state's public records

- **Treasurer/Insurance Commissioner**
  Received all moneys paid into the state treasury; paid all warrants drawn by the comptroller on the state treasury; kept detailed records of all transactions involving the state's money; and handled insurance matters related to his duties as Insurance Commissioner.

- **Attorney General**
  The chief legal officer, and headed the Department of Legal Affairs. The

attorney general rendered legal opinions at the request of state government agencies and appeared on behalf of the state in all suits in the District Courts of Appeal and the Supreme Court in which the state has an interest. The department provided all legal services required by any department unless otherwise provided by law. It defended the state on appeals from criminal convictions through state and federal courts. The department provided assistance to local law enforcement agencies in major felony cases and maintained regional offices throughout the state to aid in these services.

In 1972, representatives from the Department of the Interior, Nixon, and their environmental partners worked together to create legislation. They visited Senator Jackson's office and introduced it to him. Jackson agreed to go along with their plan rather than his own. He announced the new bill to Congress and proclaimed that he and Senator Lawton Chiles were to be cosponsors, together with two republicans, Senator Ed Gurney of Florida and Senator Gordon Allott of Colorado.

In February, Nixon addressed the Senate Interior subcommittee at a hearing. He planned the purchase of half a million acres of swamp land and appropriated millions of taxpayer dollars to carry out the task. According to the bill, the state of Florida and the federal government would work together to achieve all goals. The state would give up land and money to go with federal funding. Nixon did not stop at Florida in his speech; he went on to propose more legislation to take land in San Francisco Bay and the establishment of eighteen new wilderness parks. He then insisted that the secretaries of agriculture and interior speed up their identification of land in the eastern United States. After his proclamation of taking land, he announced an executive order requiring development of regulations to control the use of off-road vehicles.

Many Ochopee landowners railed their elected officials at a meeting in April. Facing the group of angry citizens, the response from Florida's governor, Reubin Askew, seemed totalitarian:

Acquisition by the federal government is the only sure way. Priority should be given to acquisition of those lands north and south of the Tamiami Trail and adjacent to the Everglades National Park and the jetport site.

He then recommended a program of cooperative management between the federal and state governments to control hunting, fishing, and any other recreational activities. Collier County manager, W. H. Turner, told the commission:

> The committee should not take any action for land acquisition until an Interior Department study of the watershed is completed. The study, which cost taxpayers three million dollars, would be wasted if congress went ahead with their plans without referring to it.

> Collier County officials know the potential benefits of the park, and we are interested in water and its conservation.

Later that year, acts passed through government gave officials of a new Florida state land-planning committee the power to pick and choose any piece of property that they so desired. These plots of land were then given a status of "an area of critical state concern." The state cabinet and governor told the planners to declare the Big Cypress an area of concern, and to create laws to control Florida land use. One of five state planners, Robert Rhodes, descended from a position as an aide to the house speaker, Richard Pettigrew, to join the group.

———————

President Richard Nixon made a statement in a speech delivered in 1973, supporting the buying up of the south Florida land. A week later, Congress found out that although Nixon seemed in favor, he did not want to use any funds toward the project for at least eighteen months. Assistant Interior Secretary Nathaniel Reed sided with Nixon and assured the committee that waiting until 1975 would cause no issues. Askew countered that delaying would increase the cost of buying the land. He then criticized the president for the delay. Senator Gurney, a republican and cosponsor of the bill, defended Nixon against the democrat.

Askew reached out for Senator Chiles' help and launched his head-start plan. In June, the Senate approved forty million dollars of Florida taxpayer money to take the land. Voting against the plan, Senator Charles H. Weber, a republican from Fort Lauderdale said, "State acquisition of Big Cypress would put off limits an area bigger than two-thirds of the counties in Florida."

Democratic senator Bob Graham, from Miami Lakes, Florida, became the manager of the new bill. Ignoring his voters of nonnative descent, Bob told the Senate, "The plan for acquiring Big Cypress protects the Seminole Indians living there. The Indians will be allowed to continue living in the area."

In June, Rhodes received a promotion to chief of the state's land-planning bureau. The eleven person group designed regulations to control Florida land development. At Naples hearings the staff informed the citizens of their future. The planners' first goal involved adding a million more acres around the existing swamp. Met with intense hostility and opposing views from every angle, they decided to put this plan on hold. In an interview with Rhodes that October he said, "We will begin to move into *monitor and enforcement* of the law in the next months. It's going to be an epic battle."

September 7, 1973. Over seven hundred landowners met for a third hearing on the land control by the planners. With the majority in opposition, tempers rose and anger swelled amid a roaming police force that monitored the crowd. Ochopee citizens and community leaders (Forrest Harmon, Daniel Whichello, Ken Weimer, Raymond Wooten and others) attended. The topic concerned the future of the Big Cypress and was hosted by Rhodes. Both Rhodes and his director, Earl Starnes, explained to the people about the various laws used as justification for taking land in possession of the attendees.

September 8, 1973. On the opposite side of the state at a Miami Beach banquet, members of the state cabinet stepped up to receive awards from an environmental group called the Florida Wildlife Federation. Conservationist of the Year Award went to Attorney General Robert L. Shevin. The Wildlife Conservation

Award went to Comptroller Fred O. Dickinson for efforts in acquiring land in 1972. State Representative Marshall Harris and State Senator Richard Pettigrew also accepted awards.

September 18, 1973. In Tallahassee, Forrest Harmon attended a hearing as a landowner but also as a member of the county's Water Management Advisory Board. He met with the director of state planning, Earl Starnes, to help him better understand the water needs of the community and the developments that existed in Ochopee. Various members of government came to the meeting, including Representative James Lorenzo Walker of a Naples district as well as developers such as Norman Herren of the Collier Development Corporation and Daniel Whichello, Ochopee motel owner. The men engaged in casual conversation with a sense of goodwill. When Starnes made mention that the current state plans would devalue land in the Big Cypress Area of Critical Concern by 50 percent, the men asked if they could see the final copy. Starnes told them that Rhodes had the document, and he was taking it to the commission meeting on the following day, so it was not available.

The next day, the Collier County Commission met in Naples, alongside their newest member, Commissioner Ruth Van Doren. The commissioners seemed to keep the people's best interest at heart, but Doren came to them as an opposing outsider from the start. Her keeping close ties with the planning chief, Rhodes revealed her intentions to the commission and the landowners. When the news of acreage being devalued reached the rest of the people, they felt outraged. Ruth Van Doren then accused all of the men who had talked with Starnes of lying. When the people heard that Doren had accused the men, sixty of them called Representative James Lorenzo Walker and expressed their anger. Doren later testified in front of the senate, urging them to take the Big Cypress. Landowners felt betrayal and insult from Doren's actions, words, and presence in their local government. Far out in the Everglades swamp, a group of irate citizens built an effigy of Ruth Van Doren, hung it from a tree, and burned it.

SAVING OCHOPEE

President Nixon's first four-year term neared its close, and he faced the next election in November of 1972 to gain four more years in office. His desperation for winning led him to carry out a variety of unethical tactics, proving the reality of his character. He ordered electronic surveillance on the White House and hired men to break into the Democratic National Committee headquarters at the Watergate hotel, and office complex in Washington DC. The burglars looked for evidence to discredit Nixon's democratic opposition. After the police caught some of the men, an investigation into the event seemed to point to Nixon's participation.

When the House Judiciary Committee passed three articles of impeachment in July 1974, and the Supreme Court ordered the release of White House tapes that appeared to implicate the president further in Watergate, he decided to resign on August 9, 1974. Even though he was entitled under the Constitution to a trial, he said that he did not want the nation preoccupied with Watergate for months to come. His work on acquiring the Big Cypress-once hoped to help with reelection goals by showing him to be an environmentally friendly president-in the end provided him no sympathy for his actions.

End of July 1975. The five Collier County commissioners, landowners, and other officials met in Naples to discuss the issue of Ochopee. Four square miles of the village surrounded its irrigation-shed post office and historic heart. It contained a handful of businesses and the most developed and valuable land. The county received a sizable portion of tax revenue from the small area. All of the men voted to authorize commissioner chairman, Stephen Mitchell, to sign a resolution asking for the four miles to be excluded from the Big Cypress takeover. County attorney David Bruner drafted two resolutions: one for Ochopee's exclusion; one asking for federal reimbursement to the county for the taxes lost during the next five years

51

if the exclusion was not granted. Called *Collier County's federal legislative delegation*, government men assigned to that county to handle the land taking and organize the National Park Service to carry it out received the last-effort plea. Copies went to Secretary of the Interior Rogers C. B. Morton, Senator Lawton Chiles, Senator Richard Stone, and Representative L. A. Bafalis.

A week later, national park, Big Cypress, land officer James Sewell appeared before the commission. With years of taking under his belt in the north of the country, he was placed by government leaders at the forefront. In Naples, he established a temporary office to begin his work. Landowners came to the meeting as well in order to discover Sewell's intentions for them. They wanted to know right away about the fate of Ochopee.

"It will be some time before my office gets to purchasing land in the Ochopee area because we will concentrate first on the sections of land of 640 acres or larger," said Sewell. A commissioner then asked him about the loss of tax revenue, and he responded, "Because the purchase is a long-term project, the tax loss to the county will be gradual."

At the meeting, the county planning staff made recommendations for development of the four square miles and asked about its exclusion. Sewell gave no clear answers, so Chairman Stephen Mitchell said, "I will ask Governor Askew's assistance to get the Ochopee area excluded from the Big Cypress purchase." Sewell responded, "Washington is the proper route to take. One of your legislators must submit a bill amending the original bill. This is the only way you can do it."

Sewell gave them no hope and little information. Frustrations rose in the room until Raymond Wooten shouted at Sewell, "I've got my whole life's work out there!" He faced the real possibility that all might be lost. Many in the room questioned the future. No one knew if they should improve their properties and continue their projects while the county questioned what to do with their draft of a zoning plan.

Mid-August. The commission continued to grapple with what to do about Ochopee. They hoped for the federal government to honor their request. With no answer, they could not decide on whether to continue to plan or if their efforts would be thwarted from the community's demise.

"We should create a zoning plan to allow landowners to develop their property to the highest possible use," said county commissioner Russ Wimer. Commissioner David C. "Doc" Brown agreed, but the other three felt concern about land price inflation that might cause speculation.

"I'm sure that Congress will honor the requests of the county commission to exclude the land from the federal purchase area," said Brown. "There will always be an Ochopee."

"The owners in the area should not be forced to stand still for the next few years while the National Park Service gets around to buying their land," said Wimer.

Owner of the Ochopee Golden Lion Motor Inn, Daniel Whichello, said:

> The secretary of the interior can change the boundaries of the pre-
> serve by seventy-eight thousand acres. That decision is expected
> October 11 at the Washington DC, hearing. Also, Ochopee has
> never been in the Big Cypress Critical area of State Concern. The
> state has never been a factor in whether or not the zoning plan
> should be approved.

The commissioners and the planning director (Neno Spagna) continued to argue over the zoning plan, but at the end of the meeting, they agreed to complete it.

"I have no confidence that Congress will exclude Ochopee from the purchase area," said Spagna. "I think it's history."

OIL

Fort Myers republican, Representative L. A. "Skip" Bafalis, read the resolution sent to him by the Collier County commissioners. November 1975, he discussed the side of the people with a subcommittee of Washington leaders.

> One-third of Collier County's taxable land is being removed from its tax rolls by the Big Cypress purchase by the National Park Service, coupled with the thirty-five thousand acres already lost to the rolls by the Everglades National Park. Federal lands will drain one million from the county's revenues. This county is particularly hard-hit by a decreased tax base as a result of publicly-owned lands.

After assessing the opinions of the law-makers, he then sent a letter to the county commission in Naples. In the letter, Bafalis wrote that moving the western boundary back to the Turner River road could not happen, because this action was opposed by Governor Reubin Askew, the secretary of the interior, and the chairman of the house interior committee. He did mention that in the talks, he felt that there might be some chance of excluding four square miles of Ochopee. The matter, he said, was still under consideration by the Department of the Interior.

The Department of the Interior, the governor, and his cabinet did not approve of removing any land from the proposed Big Cypress Preserve while perpetuating a message of conservation of water, land, and animals. Then in the spring of the following year, six oil companies met with the cabinet for an approval of seventeen new wells in the area designated for the preserve. James T. Williams of the Bureau of State Lands said, "We certainly need more exploration to discover our mineral resources, and if it can be done without damage, the state should proceed." The cabinet and the governor then approved the drilling for oil for fifteen sites. Exxon proposed an eleven-mile access road off of the Tamiami Trail that cut across the sawgrass to well sites right through the middle of the Big Cypress. The cabinet also approved this road. Hunters and outdoorsmen objected to running heavy equipment across the swamp, blazing trails in the once-virgin territory.

Florida Government at the time

Governor:	Reubin O'Donovan Askew
Commissioner of Agriculture:	Doyle Conner
Commissioner of Education:	Ralph D. Turlington
Comptroller:	Gerald Lewis
Secretary of State:	Bruce Smathers
Treasurer/Insurance Commissioner:	William D. Gunter
Attorney General:	Robert L. Shevin

Exxon drilled in areas known as Sunniland and Felda, north of Ochopee, for years, but the company committed several millions of dollars to the exploration of the Big Cypress. Once they discovered oil in the test wells (the first being a gusher), the governor and cabinet ordered them capped and closed, and then told the public that no oil was found.

Community leaders organized in Ochopee at the local restaurant of the Golden Lion Motor Inn. George Karth, owner of Ochopee Gas Company, told a reporter:

> They say we're an ecological hazard, then they let the oil company come in. Oil company says that they didn't find oil. But I know they did. They have thirteen wells, and they capped them, just waiting until they got rid of all of us so we can't scream.

Daniel Whichello and Forrest Harmon appeared on the Naples television news to inform the public about the frustrations of being forced to fight for their freedom of land use against the over-dominant government and their new policies. These Ochopee men went on to expose the attempts to hide oil discoveries. They then faced the brunt of anger from both the state planners and the politicians at later meetings.

LAND COMMISSIONS

In US history, government took private land for important and vital reasons: such as to house troops during wartime or for expanding the railroad system. In 1791, the fifth amendment to the US Constitution helped protect the people from abuse by stating, "-nor shall private property be taken for public use, without just compensation." Cases existed in Big Cypress where landowners gave up their property for the price offered, and much of the half-million acres came under government control without consequence. Some people bought swamp land, with no chance of development, their property being in places submerged in water and unreachable by road. With anxious energy, they abandoned the acreage to the purchase. Some hunters agreed that having the park service maintain the swamp kept future developers from ruining it, not knowing that decades later they would be pushed out as well, losing freedoms and rights to hunt on this land.

Even in Ochopee, people here and there with smaller plots gave up and moved without complaint. But hundreds of people in the Big Cypress refused low-ball prices offered to them by the land acquisition. These citizens felt that the reason for making landowners move was unclear, and not legal or constitutional. In many cases these owners had a big stake and investment in the land, whereas the government men had none.

A controversial tactic of the government used in the Big Cypress takeover was the use of the commission system. Invented with the purpose of helping poor farmers in the Tennessee valley area with legal matters of land, it allowed for a temporary court. Farmers did not have to travel long distances as the court came to them. In the 1970s and 1980s, government officials used this system in an unjust manner. Each owner deserved a jury of their peers and proper representation.

Attorney General Robert L. Shevin mailed a barrage of letters telling people that they did not need a lawyer. It stated that they could come to court by themselves and have their case presented to the commission-a panel of three judges. Individuals not in agreement with the first price offered came to court, but the commission held off all cases with representation for years while they processed people without lawyers. One by one, the defendants came to the court, arriving with their land assets, and leaving without them. The government whittled away at the Big Cypress with each swing of the gavel. One man who drank at the Golden Lion bar felt so distraught about losing his land that he left, and in his misery failed to notice a Trailways bus that killed him on impact. Other people resorted to anger, to try to fight back.

When a ranger left his Wrangler Wagon parked to go inspect the locally owned trailers in the woods for evidence of people returning to their lost property, someone destroyed the vehicle with an automatic assault rifle. Still others called for the assassination of some of the politicians and organizers of the legislation, which included Browder. A good amount of people attended the hearings, talked with government representatives, raised money, and went to Washington, DC, hoping that playing by the rules might accomplish something.

Representatives for the government-and many of the citizen supporters of the legislation-never lived in Ochopee, nor did they invest years of time, work, and money on a piece of land with the results being livelihoods to feed their families. Instead, politicians installed laws to grab land; state planners designed to devalue it; and park service officials took inventory of usable buildings, while the Ochopee community continued under their shadow.

NPS AND ALRA

Some of the most life-loving people lived and worked among the ranks of the National Park Service. Americans looked to them for guidance, expertise, and education to help them navigate the natural world, feel safe, and discover appreciation.

In the Miami hearing of 1971, a small segment of the crowd chanted, "Take their Land, take their land!" It was natural behavior for people living on the properties-or trying to make a living and a life-to feel angry.

Whether caused by big-picture-minded politicians not concerned with the details of their legal achievements or through overzealous environmental lawsuits, National Park Service policy changed. Over the last thirty years and into the future, Non-land-owning citizens gave their money, time, and opinion to form organized environmental groups-which contributed to a modern civil war. Like all wars, the innocent became the victims. The creation and promotion of overburdening legal policies were aimed at protecting nature, but excluded people as being part of that world, and thus led to hundreds of human rights violations.

> My great grandpa was able to keep his place, for as long as it stood, without being allowed to fix anything. Barely a year went by, and they got tired of waiting. Leon took the family to Everglades City to get supplies (it took a day to get there and a day back, with their chug-a-lug-powered liter). While they were gone, rangers went to the house and set it on fire. Suffice it to say, there's no love lost to the Park Service. -George Hamilton

In 1849, Congress created the United States Department of the Interior to oversee domestic matters. Responsibilities included taking care of the water and jail system for the nation's capital, Washington, DC. For the nation, the interior managed public parks, hospitals, and universities as well as exploration of the western wilderness, which led to the creation of wagon routes for settlers. Having discovered abundant land, the department set some territory aside and created the first National Park: Yellowstone. In 1879, the organization created the United States Geological Survey. This agency was composed of experts on land examination and provided studies and surveys of mineral and geological resources-such as oil and gas-for the country. In 1916, American president Woodrow Wilson put in place the National Park Service to oversee the thirty-five parks and monuments created by that time as an agency under the Department of the Interior.

Throughout the century, the National Park Service evolved into specialized divisions of tens of thousands of employees. Tasked with the service of interpretation, park rangers assisted visitors to the government-maintained land with information about weather forecasts, trail, lake, and river locations, and education about wildlife. In the coming decades, the organization increased its responsibility from simple land caretaking to medical, rescue, and firefighting. Then in the 1970s, government aimed public funds at paying for the training of many agents in law-enforcement and their regular use of firearms. Park-service management and politicians defined an assortment of legislation to dictate and control the actions of all people visiting the *government's* land-including Big Cypress.

A tool used for revenue generation, the permit, applied to all aspects of citizen life within the held territory. Government attained the right to rental payments and royalties on oil, gas, and mineral production in 1920, but with modern-day permits, they collected on camping, hunting, hiking, and canoeing. Additional law bound the freedom of artists and film makers from using the beauty of the public land in their work for sale without payment to the government for special permissions. Rather than stopping with legislation at preventing the removal of rare orchids for overseas breeding or the taking of baby alligators to sell as pets, government added more law, forbidding removal of anything: such as a dead branch used as a walking stick, a fallen flower from a tree, or the useless shed skin of a crawfish.

Recently, the Park Service landed helicopters and surrounded two camps in Alaska with men armed with guns. No shots were fired, but a lot of scared people were involved. It turns out that no one in the camps had done anything wrong, but over-aggressive behavior by the park service has stirred up a hornet's nest in Alaska. You should know that the park service has its own version of a "swat" team. The teams, armed with shotguns and automatic weapons, are called "special events teams" There are three (in the San Francisco area, the South, and the East), and they come completely equipped with riot gear. Just last year, one was called out to handle a demonstration in Big Cypress (Florida). We share your wonder as to why the park service needs a "swat" team. -Chuck Cushman, 1980 *Inholders Newsletter*

Charles S. Cushman's father worked as a ranger for the National Park Service at the Pioneer History Center in Yosemite. As a young man, Chuck volunteered with the group in 1959, and later, his son also worked for the NPS. Throughout the years, Chuck became involved in various conservation groups, but through the 1970s, he witnessed numerous abuses against landowners as they suffered at government intrusion in their private lives. These people (who resided in the middle of or near government land) were considered "Inholders" by the NPS. In 1978, Chuck signed on to help with a new human rights organization called The National Park Inholders Association.

The organization fought to protect Americans from unwanted property acquisition. Back in Yosemite from 1977 to 1980, people and the park went head-to-head with director William Whalen leading the attack. During his leadership, the service morale dipped to an all-time low, as many of the regional senior people began quitting. A year before, he displayed arrogance at the National Concessionaires Congress, when he told the attendees that he planned to move most of the buildings that the concessionaires used to the park perimeter. Congressman and house Interior Committee Chairman, Morris Udall, called for Whalen's removal in January of 1980. Then Interior Cecil Andrus fired him in April.

NIA (National Inholders Association) felt that Whalen was a powerful puppet for Congressman Phil Burton, Chairman of the Parks Subcommittee in the house, and he was being made a scapegoat in time for the senate oversight hearings, which will bring into focus the pressure tactics being applied in the present land-acquisition process. -*Inholders Newsletter*

The following, showing other agency abuse, was reprinted from a May 1980 article.

Abuse in Big Sur

Dennis McClung of Big Sur, California, purchased two parcels, ten and 70 acres, of land in Big Sur several years ago. Last spring he developed a severe back problem, requiring specialized surgery out of the country. In order to pay for the surgery, McClung offered a portion of his property for sale to the Forest Service. The agency was very interested in the offer as McClung's property was adjacent to a wilderness area in Los Padres National Forest. McClung went through endless negotiations with the Forest Service; each time reaching what he thought was agreement, only to have Forest Service personnel return weeks later with additional demands. The agency continually insisted it needed a little more land, a little more public access, a trail site, and so on. Meanwhile, McClung had a medial deadline to meet. And he made the mistake of telling the Forest Service of his need for cash. The Forest Service decided it wanted all 70 acres of McClung's parcel in order to close the deal, taking away McClung's land and his dream of building a home on his property. We suspect the Forest Service deliberately delayed and renegotiated agreement for the purpose of forcing McClung to sell all of his property.

1980. The National Park Inholders Association changed its name to the National Inholders Association to better represent their cause of helping to protect people from all government agencies and environmental group land abuses.

June:

> Joe Picklener, former deputy chief of the legislative division of the
> National Park Service and present superintendent of Fire Island
> National Seashore in New York, admitted in an interview with
> the Fire Island Tide that it was a National Park Service policy to
> condemn all private land within a park, forcing Inholders to give
> up their land.

In 1995, the NIA became the American Land Rights Association, ALRA, and possessed twenty-six thousand members located in fifty states. Chuck Cushman continued to lead the group into present times as executive director. Since the start he has:

> Written numerous articles on inholder rights; lectured at col-
> leges and universities; appeared as an expert guest on *Late Night
> America*, *Today* on NBC, *All Things Considered* on public radio,
> CNN, CBS, ABC and NBC news; been a subject of segments of
> *60 Minutes*, *The News hour* with Jim Lehrer and *CNN Presents*; has
> been featured in numerous national magazines regarding land-use
> issues; appeared as guest speaker before hundreds of multiple-use
> and private-property advocacy groups and political-interest orga-
> nizations. -ALRA website

He described the group as:

> A public interest advocacy organization that works to protect
> landowners across America who are affected by various growth
> management schemes as well as the Endangered Species Act,
> Clean Water Act (wetlands), and other Federal land-use regula-
> tory laws.

Their mission statement:

> ALRA and its members are dedicated to the wise-use of our re-
> sources, access to our Federal lands and the protection of our pri-
> vate property rights.
>
> ALRA's efforts are pro-people, not anti-park. Parks and wilder-
> nesses can be positive and should be established where they do not
> damage the socioeconomic. -ALRA Website

This human rights group helped thousands of people over the last thirty years to fend off attacks on their land, families, and American way of life. They revealed to victims solutions in the legal realm as well as comfort in their personal struggles to defeat oppression and regain normalcy.

Please see the Resources Chapter in the back of the book for information about contacting the ALRA for assistance with land issues involving the government. They are experienced and ready to help.

Popular bumper sticker from the early 1980s

GAO

The Budget and Accounting Act of 1921 created The General Accounting Office and placed it under control of the comptroller general and deputy comptroller general. The agency assisted Congress and its members in performing their legislative and over-sight responsibilities. Nonpolitical and independent, the GAO of the legislative branch carried out legal, accounting, and auditing for federal government operations and made recommendations for effectiveness and efficiency. Informed of the Interior Department's controversial land-removal process affecting the United States, the GAO began an investigation. In May of 1978, they sent a report to Congress, titled *Federal Protection and Preservation of Wild and Scenic Rivers is Slow and Costly.*

The following year, another report was released, titled, *The Federal Drive to Acquire Private Lands Should be Reassessed.* The report analyzed eight parks over the course of most of a year, and read:

> The National Park, Forrest and Fish and Wildlife Services had been following a general practice of acquiring as much private land as possible regardless of need, alternative land-control methods, and impacts on private landowners.

> The federal government already owns well more than one-third of the nation's land, and the committee believes that the current drive to acquire still more should be reassessed. Too often, it seems, federal land acquisition is seized upon as a quick fix for recreation, resource conservation, preservation, and environmental-protection proposals. Meanwhile, the rush to bring more and more acreage

into federal ownership has at times trampled upon individual property rights, vastly inflated land values, and in some cases, fostered profiteering and corruption. Preliminary findings from a current General Accounting Office investigation have suggested widespread problems in this area and seriously questioned the real need for many land-acquisition proposals and practices.

Clearly, in the committee's judgment, the availability of more than $220,000,000 in unused appropriations diminishes the need for more new funding in fiscal 1980.

The National Park Service took offense to the criticism and claimed innocence to all of the deeds accused of them. They did not agree that landowners held legitimate concerns for the land-acquisition process. The GAO then returned to their report and added additional pages, and then they recommended to Congress to place a moratorium on all land acquisition to stop all further taking.

The human rights organization, National Inholders Association, revealed in a 1980 newsletter:

The GAO report is independent evidence by congress's own investigations that confirms what you have been saying for several years: that the park service does not look at alternatives to fee title in acquisition; that it buys too much land while not paying attention to inflation; damages local governments by reducing the tax base; and does not pay attention to the general socio-economic damage caused by its actions; is unconcerned about the financial and emotional costs of relocating thousands of families, many of whom have lived on the same land for several generations. Relocation benefits are often held over an inholder's head.

Many sellers are left substantially poorer after the purchase than before, but the law says they should be even.

Little or no attention is paid to the transfer trauma of being forced off your land and out of your homes.

Tenants are shortchanged and forced from their homes with little in the way of benefits to help them.

Big Cypress:

In March of 1981, the Senate held hearings into the land-acquisition policies and practices. During the hearings, some environmentalists suggested tighter controls and more condemnations of family homes. By June, the Department of the Interior possessed 88 percent of the proposed acquired property. Months later, at a meeting in Tallahassee, an interior official assured Florida Governor Bob Graham that completing the 1,200 condemnation cases in progress finished off 98 percent of the land. Graham and other officials voiced their concern about the remaining ten thousand acres. They wanted that land as well. They wished to be informed of any changes to the plans for the Big Cypress or any national park or preserve in the country. The official took the demands back to Interior Secretary James Watt.

OHIO

Officials condemned the home of Ken Weimer and his wife, Jeanie in Big Cypress. The two were forced to fight their government in Tallahassee. At that same time, their home state faced a similar battle.

The following excerpts were extracted from a Frontline television special produced and directed independently by Mark and Dan Jury and produced for Frontline by Stephanie Kepper: "For the Good of All."

> "They are taking these homes, because in the mind of some bureaucrat, it would be better to remove them and have open space, than have a family living there, paying taxes, and raising their children there!" said Leonard Stein-Sapir, the president of the Homeowners Association in Cuyahoga Valley.

His voice blasted across the crowded meeting room of residents under threat of losing their homes. Congressman John Seiberling who wrote the legislation, attended the meeting as well. Residents of the Ohio Valley inhabited just 2 percent of a proposed national recreational area, spanning thirty-two thousand acres of wilderness. The families living in the five hundred homes needed the land to survive, and with enough space to sustain them and the overwhelming majority of animal and plant life, government chose to remove only the people. Days after Seiberling's legislation passed in 1974 and after Nixon's speech to take land for parks, the National Park Service began the acquisition process on the first house. A man whose home resided in the valley, Seiberling, first told his neighbors:

> We're not just talking about the conservation of a piece of land;
> we're talking about the conservation of people as well. In planning
> the park, the people must be considered a resource, along with the
> trees and flowers, the birds, and the waterfalls.

These people knew and loved the nature and made extraordinary attempts to keep the surroundings intact. They agreed with the congressman and expected no issues with the buying up of all of the undeveloped property. This outcome benefited their peaceful lives, and they believed him when he said, "No more than twenty to thirty homes will be disturbed."

Congress turned the work over to the National Park Service, and so Superintendent of the Valley, William Birdsell led the effort as he believed that he was creating a park for all people, for all time, for the greater good. Congress gave Birdsell instructions and techniques for acquiring and told his organization to develop a specific plan for each step of their duties in 1974, but by 1979, no such plan existed, yet most of the homes were gone. Congress told the National Park Service to only remove people using the all-out-buy-out method in rare cases. In the majority of cases, they were supposed to use the method of a "Scenic Easement." In this technique, the owner made a deal with the government, kept their house, and became part of the park, if they promised not to make any changes to the property, thus preserving the community. The Superintendent testified under oath that year that of three hundred homes, only a few easements were allowed, one of them being given to Seiberling. Birdsell told a reporter in a television interview:

> There was never intent to protect a community. It's like any other
> public project: some people are affected for the good of all.

The reporter for a *Frontline* television special, Jessica Savage, told her viewing audience:

> The people of the valley say that the park is costing them their
> homes. The residents are not against the park, only against what

they call the destruction of their community. It is questioned whether a federal bureaucracy like the park service thwarted the will of Congress, ignored the law of the land, and overrode the rights of individuals.

Bob Lindley farmed the land for over one hundred years. Two rangers came out and told him that since he wasn't a big-time farmer, what he was doing was classified as a hobby. They said that that is the way it was, and they wanted his property.

Bill Erdos received a letter saying that they needed to send an appraiser out to appraise his property. In a phone call to the national park, he asked why, who made this determination, and for what reasons? They told him that it was because his property was on a list. The call left him with the impression that there was some mysterious higher-level person making these decisions.

A resident of the community, Burrel Tonkin, told the interviewing reporter:

> Well, I didn't quite believe it myself at first. I asked the lawyer, "Suppose we just ignore the son of bitches." He said, "Well, you can't do that." I said, "Why not?" "Because, well, they'll send armed men in to take it away from you."

Bob and Natalie Valcanoff owned a thriving flower shop in the community. Bob told the visiting reporter:

> We were angry, here we are, we've established ourselves. All of a sudden to have somebody come up and say, "Hey you gotta move; we want your property."

His wife Natalie added:

> I cry a lot. I'm bitter; I've lost a lot of weight. We were told what were supposed to get, and what we were to do, and that was it, whether we liked it or not. Well upon refusing that, we were told

that if we did not accept their offer, we could face condemnation. Ninety days is not near enough time to move a business that's been here for twenty-eight years.

The reporter asked the superintendent, Birdsell about the fate of the flower shop, and he responded:

Because of the size of that shop and its location, we don't predict any use for that at the present time; it'll be simply obliterated and become public use area, along the river there.

On moving day, the Valcanoffs began loading up all of their belongings into a truck; they lived in the house over thirty years. Natalie turned to the camera as her husband stood in the next room and said, "He's so nervous and so upset that he just-he's holding his stomach. He doesn't want to move. We have to start all over again."

An elderly woman named Clara Schmidt received an easement, but one day she was rocking in her chair, and a park ranger came up to her, pointed to a dog wandering, and asked, "Is this your dog?"

"Yes," said Clara.

"Well, he just killed a wood chuck around the corner."

"Well, the farmer that has a little garden down the road, he'll be coming up and thanking me," she said. The park ranger than charged the woman with a fine for harassing a woodchuck.

"You mean if a woodchuck comes up and starts eating our cabbage and lettuce, we can't do nothing about it?"

"No," said the ranger.

Jessica Savage reported to the viewing audience:

Unfortunately, what happened here with this park is not an isolated case. During the period when this film was shot, 1979 through

1982, thousands of families across this country had their houses and their properties turned into park land.

President of the homeowners association, Leonard Stein-Sapirs left the city to raise his family in the peaceful valley. He built his house with award-winning architecture that landed it an article in a national magazine. When the NPS sent him letters-and then visited-they expressed their need to take it away from him. One word came to mind, and he put it to them: "Why?" The horse trail they planned went through the property, they first answered, but later the story changed to having the need to preserve the open space-and to add two more acres to the already thirty thousand. They wanted to bulldoze it. Then they told him that it's possible that they might save the house and convert it into a visitor center. Leonard later expressed his feelings, after the taking and destruction of many of the homes, to a news reporter:

> They're buying homes for hundreds of thousands of dollars that they don't need, and they're bulldozing them. And it's shear lunacy. They're destroying homesteads that have been in the same hands for generations, for no reason.

> Preserving the community, would have added charm to the park; it would have lowered the cost of administration; it would have lowered the cost of acquisition. It was absolutely ludicrous for them to do this, but the park service has a mindset that all parks should be devoid of people. You can preserve trees; you can preserve birds; you can preserve woodchucks; but people have got to go.

The report shot video of landowners protesting in the city streets carrying picket signs that read, "Hell no! We won't go!"

A resident spoke into the reporter's microphone:

> We are for the original concept of the park, which was to preserve the area to keep the trees, to keep the people living here, to have

the farms maintained, to keep the village intact. That's what we're fighting for and protesting for.

On the scene at one of the public hearings, the reporter looked at the camera and said:

The residents charge the park service is coercing them out, pressuring them, into selling their homes for park land.

Over the angry crowd, Congressman John Seiberling tried to explain the government's side:

That's democracy. You'll never find in any group everybody agreeing. It's inevitable when you do something this big, that some people aren't going to want it. The primary thing is that public interest must be served. And as far as I'm concerned, my personal interest and everyone else's personal interest that lives in this valley, is secondary to the public interest.

The concerns of the several hundred people that live in this valley are very important, but the concerns of the millions of people who are going to use this park are also important.

In the summer of 1980, Leonard went to Washington, hoping to persuade the park service to stop taking houses. He met with the head of the NPS, Russell Dickenson. After the meeting, the reporter interviewed Dickenson about what happened during the conversations, and he replied:

What everybody was generally expressing was the kind of concerns that many of the home owners in the national recreation have about the future, where they are headed, and the impact of the national recreation project on their lives, and we had an exchange of views, and they have now gone on their way.

Leonard gave his opinion to the reporter concerning his view of Dickenson:

> My feeling was that this is a large corporation. The interior de-
> partment is a large corporation. He is the executive head of it.
> They have a subsidiary company in the valley, where there are a
> few problems, and he will do what he can to see if there are prob-
> lems. It was very clinical-devoid of any emotion.

For eight months, Leonard heard nothing, so he arranged a meeting with the Department of the Interior. The meeting was attended by Ric Davidge, special as-sistant secretary of interior; John McClaughry, White House advisor; G. Ray Arnett, undersecretary of the interior; Barton Craig, attorney for the homeowners association; and Tom Roush, MD and former resident who told the government officials:

> The most poignant central fact is that the people did not have to
> be kicked off their land in order to have a wonderful park. They
> could have stayed.

The valley men asked the officials to let the people in the last homes buy back their properties. The government men said that the residents would never do it, so Leonard called one couple and asked them if they would buy back their property if given the opportunity. The elderly man on the other end told him:

> We'll, you're just a little bit late; there's nothing left. First they tore
> the barn down; our neighbors told us that they came in with bulldoz-
> ers and leveled the house right down and covered up the basement.
> They just deliberately tore it down and hauled it away in trucks.

The reporter visited the family and recorded the couple on video. The wife told her:

> There's just no word to express it, the feeling it leaves you
> with. And also that our ancestors aren't here, any of them, to

see this happen, because I don't think any of them could have taken it.

Months passed, and hopes began to fade. Said Leonard, "Never heard a word, nothing-absolutely nothing."

A woman returned to her property-an empty lot bordering a wooden fence and a dirt road. She walked across the grass where she used live. In a distressed tone, full of anguish and frustration, she told the reporter:

> It's a beautiful picnic area, no question about it, but there was a home here. We never see anyone using it. Why did the home have to go? Out of thirty-two thousand acres? And it's inconceivable to me that Congress could specify in the enabling legislation that this community was to be allowed to remain here, and it just was ignored.

TIME LINE

1968   Joe B. Browder pursued Miami development politics

1968   The Miami Jetport project began

1969   Richard Nixon became president of the United States and faced the Vietnam War and an energy crisis

1969   Miami meeting between the sides of the jetport conflict

1969   Results of studies gave Nixon evidence to stop construction

1970   Senator Lawton Chiles with Joe Browder searched for support to take the cypress swamp

1971   Swamp takers gather support from Nixon by way of smiting his opponent Jackson and Nixon announced his plans in November to take the swamp.

1971   Jackson's Miami hearing

1971   December, Ochopee residents prepared to fight at a meeting in the Golden Lion diner

1972   New legislation created; a Land planning committee established to devalue the land and control its use.

1973	Florida governor Askew launched his head start plan
1973	September 7, Angry land owners met to fight the planners and save their livelihoods
1973	September 8, Awards given to politicians in Miami by an environmental group for taking land
1974	Nixon left office before being impeached
1975	Collier county commissioners try and save Ochopee's historic heart
1975	State government approved drilling for oil in the Big Cypress

Simple Life

THE BOWLING BALL GERMAN SHEPHERD

While men planned the defeat of the Miami Jetport, Daniel Whichello prepared to begin his life as a motel builder in Ochopee. He and his wife, Marge, had a six-year-old German shepherd named Brandy, who lived with them in their modular home on the edge of the swamp in Ken Weimer's community.

One day, Daniel left his bowling ball on the floor after cleaning it. Upon returning, he found the animal rolling it around the room with his mouth and nose. Then he began gripping the finger holes of the ball with his teeth and tossing it short distances. When the couple took him outside, he steered the sphere in circles for hours, until he tired, then he lay in the grass panting, with it between his front legs.

On a late afternoon, no one could find Brandy in the house or in the yard. Daniel went searching. After making the turn onto US 41 in his car, he saw what appeared to be a crumpled pile on the side of the road next to Ken's real-estate office. Recognizing it as his shepherd, he headed home and returned with a shovel. Ken emerged from the building and met him at the twisted form, which swarmed with flies. When they looked closer, Brandy looked back at them. They lifted the dog and slid him into Ken's pickup truck and then rushed the injured canine to a veterinarian hospital in Naples. The doctors saved his life, but in the end, a leg required amputation.

After a month of healing from the car accident, Brandy rose to his feet as a tripod. He swayed, and then hopped one step on the single front leg. Two back legs followed, and then he hopped again. For weeks, Daniel lifted him up and took him outside when he needed to be relieved, until his strength returned. Marge placed the bowling ball in front of the dog, and off he went driving it around the property.

Months later, with the ball in the lead, Brandy followed his family members behind the house. Daniel worked on building a shed, while Marge pulled weeds, and Brandy circled, zigzagged, and pushed the ball into the canal. The couple stopped their chores and walked over to where they found him staring at the water seemingly confused.

"Sorry, Brandy," said Marge.

In an empty field next to the house, members of the community set up picnic tables and a grill for an after church Sunday dinner. Brandy wandered between the residents and interrupted their chatter with a splash. Everyone turned their attention to the dog swimming across the canal. In his path, a dark roundish object floated, and when he reached it, jaws from an alligator came to the surface and pulled the three-legged German shepherd under, and he was gone.

People gasped at the sight. The alligator's head broke the surface, still clamped onto the struggling dog. The crowd grabbed rocks and threw them at the reptile. Kicking and biting the adversary, Brandy fought until he broke free. He made it to shore and bounded out of the water where surrounding family rushed him to the hospital.

Brandy eventually healed from the teeth wounds. He lay around the house watching the front door, and seemed to experience depression. After news of the famous gator-fighting, bowling-ball dog, spread, a neighbor bought a new ball, which he brought over to the house, and presented it to the canine. The shepherd rose up on three legs and took it on a trip around the yard.

Over the next months, Brandy kept the ball close-like a best friend. He almost never left it alone. One day, he pushed it into the canal again. He stood staring into the water, searching. He paced a little, looked some more, and then he walked away and went back into the house alone.

Brandy and his ball in Ken Weimer's community

Brandy after his leg was removed

GOLDEN LION

Where some small towns entertained gambling in bingo parlors, parades on main streets, dancing in dance halls, drinking in watering holes, and politics in moose lodges, after 1970, Ochopee's Golden Lion Motor Inn maintained an all-in-one solution to these kinds of events. Local swamp dwellers, other-country foreigners, and northern tourists mingled for parties and holidays.

For Easters, the girls in the family, Nancy and Kathy, stayed up with some of the staff all night coloring hundreds of eggs. They dried in crates across the polished steel counter tops in the restaurant kitchen. After church, Easter afternoon, over a hundred contestants searched for them in the motel stairwells, on the second floor balconies, around the pool, on window sills, in the grass, or on cars in the parking lot. Nothing was off limits. Anyone willing to hunt down an egg just needed to BYOB: *Bring Your Own Basket.* No cost was ever charged.

Most thought that the appearance of Santa Claus impossible without access to a mall or some reasonably sized establishment, but in Ochopee, Mr. Claus made an exception. Arrangements with a local swamp buggy led to his welcome appearance. Down US 41 came Santa sitting in his buggy, which rolled across the front lawn of the motel and stopped at an awaiting decorated throne. More than a hundred children came from miles to stand and wait for their turn to sit on his knee-no different from any other community in any other town.

Patrons renting a room at Ochopee's motel enjoyed a refreshing, blue pool in the midst of nowhere-a pleasant surprise for a paying customer. The owners did not believe in excluding it from the people living in the area. They offered it up to the YMCA to teach kids how to swim, the high school in Everglades City for their physical education department, and to anyone who brought their bathing suit. A private motel pool became the official public version for the southern Everglades, with not a cent charged to anyone.

One evening, someone played a prank by dropping an alligator into the pool. The next morning, two German tourists screamed when they saw the creature and dived into the office.

After dark, bar drinkers felt drawn to the pool light and found it a perfect place to continue their festivities of which skinny-dipping became an occasional event and according to a rumor at least one airboat used it for a parking lot.

Once the public pool to the Southern Everglades

The formal dining room transformed into a disco dance club on weekends and hosted live bands and drink specials. A frequent customer to the restaurant, Margie, ate there one special night. She came to the Everglades from Greenwich Village in New York City around 1950 at age twenty-two. She married into the Weeks family, who settled Chokoloskee Island, the tiny piece of land just south of Everglades City. In town, her sister (known as Mama Dot) became famous for her ice cream parlor. Margie finished eating dinner with her husband that night when she witnessed a commotion in the dining room. A local fisherman shouted angry curses because the dance act of women hired in from Miami turned out to be men. Taking the advice of a local bartender, owner Nancy booked the act. Margie left sensing trouble. Under the revolving disco ball and across a temporary stage some men exchanged blows and in the squabble, wigs flew-even one from a woman customer.

When Miami Dolphin football games did not sell out, The National Football League authorities blocked them from general broadcast in and around Miami. Located just on the other side of the forbidden range, the Golden Lion's multitude of color televisions lured people to this football haven. Tailgating-hunting-groups, social and charity organizations, and board-members from corporations bought up strips of rooms for the weekend. Seeing local people pushed out of a chance at watching the game, the management dedicated one room for football: room 101. With mirrors and furniture removed a small theater came to life and served anyone willing to pay fifty dollars. One of the owners, Ed, made sure that two girls served a full liquor bar to patrons while they enjoyed the game from their air-conditioned hideaway, free from bugs and clear of humidity and heat.

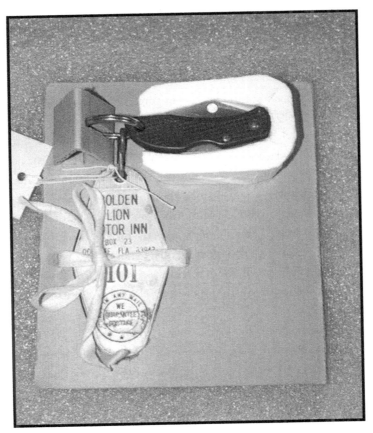

*Picture of a stolen key to the infamous room 101
courtesy of the National Park Service archives*

DRY SEASON

Summer rain drowned the swamp for months, causing the sawgrass to grow tall and dense enough to hide any lurking animal. Through the fall and into the winter, rain seldom fell, and by spring, the cold season had left a massive pile of dead vegetation. Beneath the layers, plant matter rotted with the rising temperature releasing gas into trapped pockets.

Day after day, clouds accumulated moisture, yet they continued to wait for June. Then in May of 1973, one small cloud, not in agreement, dropped some rain and stretched its muscle with a defiant strike of lightning into the ground. The resulting explosion lifted a sea of fire three feet in the air and burst the pockets into flames. Hundreds of acres caught fire-and then thousands. From over the top of the Everglades in a steel tower, a ranger spied churning smoke rising to the sky. With his radio, he sent word to the local authorities, and to the National Park Service. Their employees scrambled, but hunters, already on the scene banded together, moving to save their cabins. Gladesmen grabbed shovels and hopped aboard their swamp buggies and airboats. These experts on the terrain scoped out an area miles ahead of the raging furnace. In this spot, they cleared out brush and dug a long ditch, called a *break*.

Behind the line, they lit small fires known as *backfires*. The controlled burn ate excess fuel in hopes of starving the approaching threat. Besides these hunters, there were no fire fighters, park rangers, or military anywhere on the land possessing the speed and skill to hit this natural disaster with an effective first strike.

Within days, firefighters from all over the nation showed up for the slow season at the Golden Lion. Men with back-packs, suitcases, helmets and axes booked rooms for the week or longer, and packed the empty motel. Each morning, owners Nancy and Kathy (sisters) worked to prepare lunches for the group to take with them to the battle. Their brother Daniel refused to charge for any of the food. Weeks in to the fight, a newspaper reporter wrote:

> Reporting on Big Cypress fire, District Forester, Ken Blacker, said, "If we can hold the northeast corner, the worst of the fight will be over...it had exploded," referring to the Seminole-Collier fire, "and was burning like a furnace across seventeen thousand acres." One ranger said, "The walls of fire had us running scared."

Exhausted, soot covered firefighters stumbled into the motel each night looking for a warm meal and a quiet bed. All were accounted for except one. Trapped in the flames, he had burned to ashes sitting on a bulldozer. With no time to mourn, the next day, the group trudged back into the fray.

THE HOG

The following was taken from the personal experience of a hunter in the early 1970's, who spent most of his life living in the swamp.

The slight cool of the approaching sundown enveloped Sonny from his crouched position behind thick vegetation at the tree line of a clearing. He looked across a man-made rectangular rock pit with shear limestone sides: *Burns Lake*. Sweaty mud stains from the long hunting day covered his lean and strong twenty-three-year-old frame. With a careful stealth, learned from being raised in the swamp, he lifted his bow and placed a broadhead arrow in the notch. Eying an unaware giant boar standing at the edge of the grass, he drew back on the string. During the second he held, his mind tapped into an instinctual force before his fingers released. A precise hit knocked the wild pig on its side, and it lay in wait. Though he surged with anticipation, his stride revealed a honed confidence. A nudge with his boot verified a safe engagement, and with some effort, he pulled what he figured to be a one-hundred-fifty-pound hog around the lake to a camp of four fellow hunters. They marveled at the trophy and Sonny glanced at his watch.

"Hey, can you look after this? I want to get some dinner in Ochopee before they stop serving. I'll be back after."

They agreed.

Sonny breezed through the front doors of the Golden Lion and found a seat in the dining room. He grabbed some of the crackers from the decanter in the center of the table. While waiting for his waitress, he unwrapped and ate two packages of them.

"Hey Sonny," said a woman who appeared to be in her forties with jet-black hair drawn up in a bun. She placed a glass on the table, filled it with water, and then put a menu in his hands.

"Dotty, I'm so hungry I could eat that boar I just shot, but I don't have the strength to skin it."

"Watcha gonna have?"

Sonny turned a page in the menu and put it aside. "I'll take the special."

"Hamburger steak with gravy and potatoes it is then. To drink?"

"I got this water here but I'll take a shot of whiskey too." He opened up two more packets of crackers and ate them.

When Dotty returned to the table, she noticed that Sonny had eaten all of the crackers from the decanter. She placed the steaming food between his hands.

"Boy, you sure like those crackers," she said.

"I'll tell ya: hunting takes it out of you. I need to fill up for tomorrow. I'm going to be hunting again all day."

Sonny drove his pickup along the gravel that led into the dark woods and out to Burns, then he followed the campfire flicker. With a long, sharp knife and a flashlight, he approached the four men.

"Boar's right where you left it," said one of them.

"Thanks. Thanks a lot." He knelt down next to the game and began removing its hide.

The group conversed, enjoying the black cloak of night, and the heat from the flames.

"Shhh," said Sonny. A sound like rocks popping came from the dark-growing louder. Two of the men flipped on flashlights and beamed them into the night. They illuminated a slow-moving pickup truck. Its headlamps powered on and its engine revved, propelling the vehicle into a speedy lunge. It halted near the group, and the driver's door swung open. A tall man dressed in a uniform, made a short trot to the fireside and lit up the men with a high beam that he held in one hand. The other he placed on a holstered gun.

"It's a little late to be skinning a hog," said the stranger. Sonny looked up while holding a bloody knife.

"It's never too late to skin an animal."

"It's against regulations to shoot a hog after dark. You are not allowed to use a gun on them right now," said the ranger.

"This hog was shot a little before dark, and I left it there while I went to eat, so I didn't miss closing time at the inn."

"No you didn't," said the ranger, who walked over to the pig. He inspected the entry and exit wounds inside of the rib cage and saw the X pattern left by the arrow. He checked the shoulder height and walked around it. He knelt down, inspected it again, and walked around it.

"I killed that with an arrow. No bullet ever touched him. And he's plenty big enough."

"I still think you killed it after dark. You can't kill pigs after dark. That's against the rules."

"Yeah, we know that already," said one of the hunters.

"Well, you've been warned." The man then left the way he came.

THE CABIN

The following is a true account recorded from a gladesman who spent most of his life hunting in the Big Cypress.

Atop a four wheeled motorized machine, sixty-year-old Milo Rupert blasted deep into the Big Cypress Swamp. The bulbous knobs from his tires spun about pushing him through tunnels of overgrown foliage and flats of mud. While his hands gripped the steering, his right thumb forced the throttle open.

Behind him he left his frustrations with hope of diffusing their building pressure. Caught up in meetings with the Park Service, arguing with men with agendas for policy, and none for people, Milo thought of *why*. They wanted their domination to be complete as they argued over which trails in the swamp should or should not be designated: *correct*. By the end of the formal meeting with the environmentalists and the rangers it was clear that the men did not want anyone in their swamp and second, that he needed *to get the hell out of there*.

Milo lifted his hand from the throttle and smashed the brake with his foot causing the four-wheeler to skid to a stop. To the side of the trail another split into the thick brush. Nailed to a tree, a large sign read, *"No Trespassing, Trail Not Authorized for ORV Use."* He paused, and then under his breath muttered, "Not authorized my ass." He turned the handle bars, slammed the accelerator and jetted down the new route.

Ahead lay deep dips in the road full of water. With care he let his vehicle dive down into the pits, half submerging him. Rougher, but more challenging, this path Milo felt necessary to explore perhaps due to a natural-born pioneer curiosity. At times like these he lost track of his age.

After thirty minutes, the trail opened up into a clearing and he saw a hunting camp with a cabin. He parked, shut the machine down, and stepped onto the grassy floor of the swamp. To his ear came the slight rustling of tree branches and a distant calling of a bird. An attentive student of construction and woodworking, Milo noticed the fine craftsmanship of this building. It was not a shoddy place built in a hurried fashion for a season, this masterwork showed signs of consideration. Stepping to its front he saw etched in a dark lettering by hand across the wall, words that read, *"Thanks for Destroying our Memories."*

The front door opened on smooth hinges and Milo entered. Light permeated the half opened windows and illuminated chairs, a table, counters, and a bunk bed all made from cypress wood. These items Milo thought must have taken months to build, but then he saw the most amazing piece of them all: a decorative stone fireplace. A massive cylindrical cone was encased in a shiny ornate pattern of lines and color. Its stone chimney reached up through the roof and was painted with a perfect orange tinge. *Amazing,* thought Milo, this fireplace made from nothing other than the land itself sits here unused and unappreciated. He sat on the wooden floor and put tinder and two logs into the circular opening of the room's center piece. He then struck a match and started a fire. Leaning against the back of a chair, he watched the firelight mix the yellow, browns, and oranges of the polished painted stone. Feeling the heat from the device drying his soaked pants and shoes, he closed his eyes and let his worries drift up the chimney.

A few weeks later, Milo checked on the cabin. In a clearing before the trailhead that led to it, he saw a man and two children standing next to their parked truck. He steered the ATV towards the group, stopped, dismounted and said,

"You know something about that cabin back there?"

"It belonged to my dad," said the man.

"It sure is beautiful. You headed to it?"

"No, just got back. I was showing it to my children. Dad built it decades ago."

"Is he still around?"

"Nah, he passed, and his buddies held on to it as long as they could; two years. The Park just kicked them out last week. This'll be the last trip for me."

"Oh? Why is that?"

"Well, dad needed money to live, because he was old, and had nothing. He offered it up to his partners but they couldn't come up with the cash. Dad made a life-estate deal with the park, so he could keep it and still get the money." Milo looked down the trail.

"Now what happens to that nice cabin?"

"I'd liked to get it and pass it down to my kids, but the park wouldn't give anyone a chance to buy it. I assume the place will be left to rot." The two talked awhile, until they said good-bye, and so the stranger and his children climbed aboard the truck, closed the doors and left. Milo never saw them again, but made an occasional visit to the cabin when he passed that way.

Weeks after a fire devastated the forest, he went to the property. The only thing he saw standing in the heap of burnt wood was the ornate chimney standing alone between the trees. He paid his respects and never returned.

DAVID CARRADINE

People found Ochopee to be a great place for farming and fishing, but movie makers discovered its value as well.

1997. Joe Pesci and Danny Glover sat down to lunch at Joanie's Crab Shack after a busy day of filming a movie named *Gone Fishin'*.

1995. A movie named *Just Cause* portrayed a diverse cast of actors: Sean Connery, Laurence Fishburne, Kate Capshaw, Ed Harris, Ned Beatty, and Scarlett Johansson. Opening credits showed the name of the community and time of the murder mystery thriller, 1986, Ochopee, Florida.

It offered a unique backdrop for the 1977 film, *Thunder and Lightning*. Star of the television show, *Kung Fu*, David Carradine, and Kate Jackson one of the three stars in the television show *Charlie's Angels*, acted together in the film. The unit manager on set told a news reporter, "We've had some of the best extras we've ever used." In this adventure story, David and Kate fought with crooked moonshiners by way of car chases and fist fights, while the plot unraveled across the back country of the Everglades.

David Carradine on the set of Thunder and Lightning

Carradine walked into the Golden Lion motel lobby that spring, and Nancy (one of the six owners) recognized him from television. She had expected his arrival since members of his crew had booked rooms for the dreaded slow summer.

David went back outside and then returned, holding the leash to a small dog. After he sat at one of the tables, the companion curled up at his feet. Nancy's brother's wife, Marge, worked as a waitress and stopped to take his order. She lifted up her ticket book and looked at him with no recognition. When she saw the dog, she said, "Sir, dogs are not allowed in the dining area." David browsed the menu. At first, he did not agree, but after she refused to serve him, he took the animal from the room.

David Carradine with antagonist characters on the set

The next morning before sunrise, the first waitress on staff entered into the diner of the motel restaurant and found it empty except for one person, David Carradine. He wore a white tank top, sleeping shorts, and no shoes. Perusing a menu, he yawned and then he asked to order some food. The waitress told him that without a shirt, shoes, and pants, his order could not be accepted. He left and returned with the proper attire.

Later that day, David went for a swim in the pool. Afterwards, he exited by way of the cement steps and then walked into the formal dining room. One of the maids, Maggie and a local woman, Jeanie Weimer, watched him crossing the room, dressed in only a bathing suit.

"You can't come in here with wet feet," said Maggie. "You need to go up to your room and get your shirt and shoes on." David stopped to complain, but he saw the two women, and retreated. Jeanie laughed.

People who met Kate Jackson found her to be sweet, beautiful, and full of personality. These same people found David to be reserved, strange, and a little bit self-absorbed. Maids reported to management about his use of smoking marijuana in his room while hosting late parties. The owners knocked on his door and escorted him out of the establishment, so David took his belongings and his entourage to a motel outside of Ochopee called Remuda Ranch.

A week later, David returned to the Golden Lion, having been kicked out of Remuda Ranch. He pleaded with the owners to let him return, but they refused. In the pouring rain that day, eyewitness Kathy Williams Doster saw the disheveled actor wandering in the weather and asked if he needed a ride. He declined and continued his walk.

OCHOPEE SCOUTS

1977. Daniel's wife, Marge, wished for activities for her children, who often played in the isolation of the swamp. She heard about a meeting in Naples, concerning the expansion of the Boy Scouts of America. After attending, she volunteered to help bring them to Ochopee. She discussed the idea with Everglades City school officials, and so they sent a letter home with the students that announced a December meeting in the library for parents and their sons.

Few people showed at the meeting, and the representative from the BSA decided that not enough interest existed to start a Boy Scout troop in Everglades City or Ochopee, and it required a male volunteer to lead as Scout Master anyways. The advisor told Marge that if she took the lead, he offered support for a Cub Scout Den for younger boys like her son. It required a female leader-a "den mother." Marge went home with a handful of books and forms. Two kids and her son signed up for her den. A few meetings later, others joined, until the official pointed out that she needed another den mother in order to accept additional boys. Her sister-in-laws and some of the mothers of the children joined.

Over the next couple years, the boys earned awards for educational achievements, accepted special recognition for bravery, and honed survival skills. They learned: the motto, "Do your best," a unique handshake, the proper salute, and techniques in keeping their uniforms in order to promote self-discipline and confidence. The Cubs participated in the traditional scouting activities: *The Boat Regatta,* hand-painted, foot-long sail-boats which they raced in rain gutters; and *The Blue and Gold Banquets,* color-themed award ceremonies.

Boat Regatta

The den mothers discovered a wealth of natural beauty and education in the swamp. At one time, this land was the floor of the ocean. Sharks swam and died, and many lost their teeth. Half way to Miami, Shark Valley allowed the scouts to learn about Florida's past, while looking in the sand for teeth and fossils. On other occasions, they gathered plant species and read books on how to identify them. The kids soon gained an appreciation for nature.

On one expedition, the park service united with the scouts and taught them about ecology and the biodiversity of a section of beach sand. After placing a hula hoop in a random location, the boys investigated the variety of life inside the circle.

Park rangers teaching the scouts about the biodiversity of life

A simple mixture of flour and water made a paste that the mothers brushed onto the Golden Lion parking lot at the "Bike Rodeo." The event worked well with their limited budget, and it presented an environmentally-safe alternative to paint. The boys competed against each other, with judges determining their ability to stay inside of the lines.

A figure eight, one of many patterns used in the Golden Lion parking lot

Nine miles southwest of Ochopee resided an older established community, dating back to the 1800s and predating Naples. This small island held a handful of families, living out their lives in isolation for over a hundred years. In October of 1970, a group of residents hoped to build a park in the center of town, and so began the process of raising funds. One of the first ideas came in the form of a Halloween festival, but something more permanent took hold in 1972 with the more appropriate theme of seafood. Everglades City achieved its park, but with each passing year, its festival grew, forming traditions and showcasing the culture of its people. Natives, who helped with the first event, shared their wares, food, and custom of wrestling alligators. Out in the open, near the park, they set up a rectangular shallow pit, where a native brave battled a beast.

After the forming of the Cub Scouts in 1977, they joined the annual celebration. Profits they made from selling plants helped to buy supplies for their activities. Across the front of their booth, a banner read: *Buy a Plant, Help the Cub Scouts Grow.* Also in Everglades City, the Ochopee scouts raised money for charity. The moms roped off a mile-long track along the fishing docks. Each lap around the course earned a donation from sponsors, attained by hard-working scouts who walked door-to-door in Everglades City. One hundred percent of the money went to help fight multiple sclerosis.

With backing by state government, Exxon went after the oil in Big Cypress. To help sagging public opinion, officials invited the scouts to witness the initial drilling. Workers ran around the oil rig site in orange jumpsuits, trying to keep the massive drill steady on a platform. The children ate free snacks and sodas, provided by the company, while George Sears, a representative from Exxon, lectured the youth about the science of the industry. They then watched as the enormous drill bit punctured the ground for its maiden voyage into the earth, as a newspaper reporter snapped a photo.

In Ken Weimer's development, Den mothers and Cubs Scouts stand at attention

DANIEL

Golden Lion motel owner and eldest sibling, Daniel Whichello, stepped through a door to the office area behind the front desk and sat in a chair. A switchboard displayed rows of holes-one for each room. He looked around and set his gaze on a Seminole jacket hanging on a rack in the corner. It exploded with red, orange, black, blue, and other colors embedded in a patchwork of blocks, bars, and sawtooth designs. Chief Rainy Jim's wife sewed the coat for him as a gift and he kept it in the office to remind him of their friendship. Rainy and his Seminole family helped build the motel-restaurant, stirring the concrete and hammering the wood alongside Daniel, his father, and his brother. Rather than investing in some plastic or commercial devices, Daniel paid the natives to use their skills to build outdoor thatched structures around the pool. They visited his father's house on mornings for coffee and conversation and spent time eating meals in the diner, discussing the politics of the day. Daniel gained a sincere appreciation for their Seminole culture after being invited to their Green Corn dance by Rainy. Daniel picked up one of the long plugs attached to a thick phone cord and inserted it into the switchboard and then put his ear up to a heavy plastic yellow handset. He tested the connections out of nervous boredom while dwelling on what might become of his family business.

When the government kept hidden their plans for Ochopee, he and his accountant John Soldavini invoked the Freedom of Information Act. Daniel read the documentation showing that the officials decided from the start to take all of Ochopee and much more land beyond that. After the creation of the Florida planning division in Tallahassee, Daniel, the County Manager Turner, Forrest Harmon, Raymond Wooten and others left to meet with them. Bureau chief Robert Rhodes and less than a dozen people, who made up his staff, hosted the meeting in a local auditorium. Hundreds of concerned land owners took their turn at a microphone on the stage. When Daniel began to speak, someone cut the power. From all of his encounters with the government officials, he concluded that the peoples' opinions meant nothing to any of them anyways, so without the power of electricity, he shouted his speech with his own voice at the agency members.

Towards the latter half of the decade, the government's plans had materialized and with so many people having to leave, it seemed unstoppable. Daniel thought about their recent trips to Washington, DC, where they tried to gather support from congressmen willing to lend a hand. In the end, with little real help for Ochopee, Daniel's thoughts entertained the idea of selling everything so that the family might start over in another place and at least have a chance. He thought that if they were going to take the town they might as well take their business. Government officials in the acquisition wanted all of the homes in Everglade Shores and so after he talked with them, he received a verbal agreement that they would indeed buy his house and then buy his business. In the months following, the government stalled. Daniel and his wife Marge got close to some NPS employees who tried to find help for their situation. When one employee discovered certain information concerning other horror stories, they relayed that to the couple. When the employee's superiors discovered that their employee was becoming too friendly with Daniel and Marge, they ordered the individual to be transferred and replaced by a new person. In one case, a park service engineer with the last name Smith began helping Daniel with appraisal advice and other suggestions, but he was soon transferred to an office in Alaska. It happened so many times in that year, Daniel became suspicious. He and his CPA then took the matter into their own hands and agreed to engage in a letter writing campaign to seek help and advice.

Daniel breathed a deep sigh and closed his eyes. His father-in-law Henry returned to take back the phones. He seemed to enjoy his post as head of communications, though sometimes Daniel caught him on the line listening to customer conversations. *One of the perks of the job,* Daniel thought. He walked into the diner. From the waitress bussing section he picked up a few crumbs from a dirty plate and then headed down the hall into the empty formal dining room. On the floor, he placed the debris and then walked over to a picture hanging on the wall and made it crooked. Later he intended to revisit to see if his workers caught the changes and fixed them. Next, he wandered into the kitchen, greeted the cook, passed between the polished steel counters and ended up in the storage room, where the youngest of the sibling owners Kathy, prepared food for the evening. Next to her on the counter sat an industrial sized jar of mayonnaise.

"Shouldn't this be in the refrigerator?" said Daniel.

"No, it's spoiled. I need to throw it out."

Daniel feared the consequences of leaving this concoction unattended.

"I'll take care of it." He picked up the jar with two hands. In the diner he saw teenager, Jack Shealy, and asked him if he might give him some assistance. Jack followed Daniel through the kitchen and into the back delivery-driveway.

"Can you get that shovel there," said Daniel motioning to the corner. Jack grabbed the shovel and continued behind him. They travelled through the parking lot and over the grass next to the building. Across a short field, they made their way around the fishing pond behind the motel and walked a little farther until Daniel finally stopped.

"Why do we have to go way out here?" asked Jack.

"I don't want anyone to touch this poison." Daniel put the mayonnaise on the ground, and looked around, then pointed to a spot.

"Dig a hole right there."

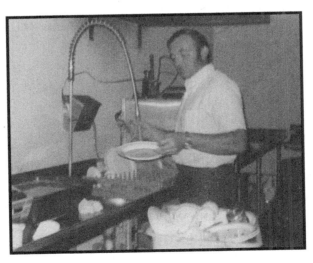

Daniel doing the dishes at the Golden Lion

MOTHER VS. NATURE

Daniel's wife, Marge, folded clothes in the laundry room at her home in Ochopee. While her husband worked at their motel, she stayed in the house to watch the youngest and third child. As for the older kids, she saw them off to school that morning and expected their return soon.

She thought of the last eight years: from being just twenty-years-old living with her parents to a mother of three in a new house and married-her dream come true. But then everything changed. *Why*, she thought, *did these government strangers want everyone to leave?* Her husband suffered nights tossing and turning and days yelling and stressing, trying to find some peace. She stood, walked into the kitchen, and paused at the basinet where her son lay sleeping off his afternoon nap. After putting the clothes on a chair, she opened the glass door to the porch. She sprayed some repellent from a can onto her arms and legs and then passed through the door to the backyard. On the far side of the screened porch, she went and looked at the garden that she had planted. A small water-melon grew next to a few tomatoes, and she saw holes in the leaves from bugs having chewed them. Gardens in the swamp seemed like uphill battles, trying to keep the bugs away. The giant orange, brown, and yellow grasshoppers-one filled the palm of her hand-struck with such aggression. They ate her rubber plants down to the roots. Though she felt admiration for the pests, and often thought of them as being beautiful. An optimist at heart, she tried to see the good even with so much bad.

Near the canal, she sat on the dock and dangled her feet over the side, averting her eyes from the glaring sun. On the opposite bank, fifty feet down river, she noticed one of the alligators lying on the edge of the bank. Still, they brought some sense of fear when she saw them-but not so much as the panic she had felt when she had first arrived. They filled her children's nightmares, while some of the neighbor's dogs succumbed to becoming alligator snacks. Unlike these giants that kept their distance, the snakes did not. She felt a shiver when she remembered one incident.

Her son learned how to draw portraits of people in Mr. Tribble's art class, and he practiced the skill one evening in the sewing room. Marge sat still while he drew her portrait. On a break from the bathroom, he returned, rigid, and speaking quickly about a huge snake that he just saw. She peeked around the corner and verified the diamond back rattle-snake as thick as her arm that wrapped around the wall and through the kitchen. Grabbing her son, she closed the door and called the police. Local deputy, Charlie Sanders, aka C. W., came to the scene and took a gardening hoe from the shed and whacked off the snake's head.

She glanced down at the minnows and sheephead gathering in the water and put the scene out of her mind. She thought of all of the animals that came into her life here in the Everglades-not all of them being a danger. She remembered the hurt baby rabbit and the injured raccoon, and then there were the two featherless black birds that her kids found on the ground, having fallen out of their nest. She nursed them *all* back to health. Then, she thought of the spiders. Once, when a water spider's egg sack broke open in the upstairs bathroom, the family spotted the giant beasts for months: at every turn on of a light, at bedtime on the ceiling, and in the closets, while picking out clothes.

From the open-screened porch, Marge heard the sound of her kids yelling.

After their afternoon snacks, her son and daughter revisited their project of dismantling the club-house. They failed to use it, and being an eye-sore were ordered to do away with it.

Marge considered that even with the downside of living in a remote location with little social interactions and having to travel many miles to go anywhere-such as a hospital or a grocery-she felt happy because of the nature and the children. She still hoped for the motel, even after all of the years they struggled to see its success. At the end of all of her thoughts, she managed to always find a bright side.

A shrill scream struck her ears. Footsteps pounded, and her children scrambled through the porch and into the house. They rushed to her and spit out their horror of a giant snake found under the floorboard of their little building. Marge jumped up, grabbed a broom from the corner and snatched a can of Raid from the kitchen counter, then ran to the backyard. Curled up in a neat, circular pile, a dark-colored cotton-mouth moccasin, waited. With the kids close behind, Marge reached the animal and whacked it with the broom then sprayed a long, hard mist of roach killer in its face. The creature uncoiled and jumped away from the dousing. It wriggled around and positioned itself for attack. It came toward Marge. With mounting adrenaline, she thought of one thing: protecting her children from harm, and so she struck by smacking it flat and spraying. The reptile sprung up, back, and teetered like a jack-in-the-box. It dropped flat on the ground, turned toward the canal, and tore off in a furious slither. The mother chased, hitting it with the broom a few more times before the snake leaped into the air and dove into the water.

Marge with a fish she caught in the canals
near her house in Ochopee

THE BAR

Ochopee entertained a few bars, such as Gator Hook and Wayside, but The Golden Lion provided a modern option. During the day, the bartender became everyone's receptionist. Orders for chickens, cows, vegetables, and jobs came through the phone line, and in some cases, people called looking for their missing significant other. The person working any given day kept a pad of paper and a pen handy at all times. Patrons knocked back drinks into the night and entered a world full of airboat races in the parking lot, fist fights across the tables, and drug use in the bathrooms. In the late seventies and early eighties, the government clamped down on landowners, clearing the woods of customers and workers. The eldest daughter, manager, and one of six owners, Nancy, felt the pinch on many occasions when she was forced to deputize a customer and set them up with a quick training on getting drinks served.

On one of those desperate nights, Nancy, and her brother, Ed, filled in for the lack of workers. Sweat poured off of the customers in the suffocating room with a broken air-conditioning unit. Nancy convincing a repair person to come to the middle of the swamp proved a near-impossible and expensive achievement for her failing business. The crawling heat pushed the drinkers to order more in hopes of blocking the misery, but instead, it fueled anger and dehydration.

Malcolm Smith perched on his barstool and looked around at his unhappy friends. He saw a puny fan pumping hot hair around the room and then thought of something.

Customers nick-named Nancy "The Little General" for her reputation of running a tight ship and not putting up with any nonsense. She was a girl around thirty-years-old and stood four feet eleven inches tall. She did the hiring and firing, ran the kitchen, and when she had to, tended the bar. Usually when she evicted a customer, she ordained them with a time limit. Whether two weeks, a month, or longer, after that, she forgave, forgot, and welcomed them home, but the plan did not always go well. Her brother Daniel on occasion bumped into a violator in town. By the end of their conversation, Daniel lifted the sentence and recruited himself a new drinking buddy. The "General" was not happy.

That steamy evening when the air-conditioning died, Nancy and Ed did their best to please the people, but for some, there was just no pleasing.

The front door slammed against the back of the wall, and hurricane-force winds exploded into the room. Napkins, glasses, bottles, menus, and everything else took flight and pummeled the patrons before clattering into a mess along the back of the building. A giant airboat fan that filled the doorway vanquished the heat in an instant. Ed shouted over the roaring engine for Malcolm to get his airboat out of there. When Malcolm moved the machine, he yelled back, "I'm going to put this into the pool!" Ed returned with

"That's going to be my airboat if you do that!" Instead of heading for the pool, Malcolm aimed for the open highway. He drove the craft across the parking lot, leaving behind a fury of hot sparks. After jumping the bank and landing in the water, the boat's rumbling motor diffused into the darkness, and Malcolm went home.

Nancy, "The Little General," in a Halloween costume

Gator Hook Lodge, by Charles Knight

My brother Jack Knight Jr. bought an old wooden building from the town of Sweetwater for one dollar. The town had been using it as a youth center and Boy Scout meeting hall. They built a new block building and were going to demolish the old one when Jack offered to move it to the Glades and use it as an outpost and sundry store. That was back in 1956. He owned a few acres on the Loop road in the Big Cypress swamp. After trucking the building to the site he had to wait for the dry season in order to build pillars to which he could place the building atop. Once that was done, fill was brought in from the rock pit at Pinecrest and used as a parking lot. Hunters and weekend warriors along with tourists and more were regulars at the store called Gator Hook. You could purchase beer, ice, and bait. Mosquito repellent and burgers too. As time went on he put a couple of picnic tables in the store for folks to relax on, to get in out of the heat and cold. As it happened he realized that his biggest sales were in cold beer and fast food so he eventually did away with the groceries and bait. Soon he added more tables and a bar. Then a jukebox and a band stand. Country music was soon played by many every weekend. I spent many a night sleeping on the floor after the place had closed. Getting up early in the morning to hunt deer, turkey, and whatever was in season with my brother and father. Gator Hook soon became Gator Hook Lodge even though there were no rooms to lodge in. Every weekend was a whirl-wind of activity and music. Hunting season saw a packed bar on most days and nights. Eventually my brother and his wife moved to Central Florida and bought a full liquor bar. My oldest sister Joyce and her hus-band bought Gator Hook and kept it in the family. They increased the menu and installed a mobile home directly adjacent to the bar. Business grew by leaps and bounds. We had a regular stable of musicians that played on the weekends that included Ervin Rouse, the composer of the Orange Blossom Special. Eventually my father Jack Sr. retired as chief of police in Sweetwater and wanted to move to the Glades full time. My sister and her husband traded the bar to dad for a house he owned in town. That's when I went from a part time resident of the Glades to full time. In the mid-70s the National Park Service wanted our land and all surrounding land to become part of The Everglades National Park. Up until that time one could travel a few miles through the Big Cypress until you came to the boundary. The NPS made offers to all the land owners. Take what we offer and continue to live on the property until you find another place to live or we can condemn the land and take it under the eminent domain act. In 1977 dad sold Gator Hook and our land to the NPS. He was diagnosed shortly after with stomach cancer and passed away less than a year later. We were told (as many were) that the NPS would erect posts or signage telling the history of the Glades settlers in the Big Cypress but in reality they had no intention of doing any such thing. They have since done everything they can to erase a rich and colorful history that should be preserved for people to be able to read about and visit. I certainly understand the need to preserve the lands in their natural state yet fail to see the logic in the decimation of true history.

Casualties

THE MONDAY MORNING
RUMOR ASSOCIATION

In 1978, two reporters returned to their offices at a New York City newspaper after a long exploration into tropical Florida landscapes. They gathered notes from interviews detailing the controversy surrounding a tiny community deep in the swamp. They wrote:

> Not a day goes by now that one of the Golden Lion's waitresses doesn't tell a story about "seeing one of Sewell's people talking to the lady from Detroit who's got those three acres of scrub back of Ma Watson." George and the friends at the table will open the *Miami Herald* to items beginning with phrases like, *"Federal officials today report they have acquired 72 percent of the Big Cypress National Preserve. This represents considerable progress."* With each story like that, the breakfast table at the Golden Lion gets a little bit closer to a bunker.

A burly man with biceps like a sailor, George Karth sat drinking coffee among his friends: Frances Watson, Forrest Harmon, Raymond Wooten, Daniel Whichello, Ken Weimer, and others. They gathered around a large wooden round table in the far corner of the diner.
George spoke:

> They're offering me thirty-four cents on the dollar. No way I'm selling at that price-and forget the relocation business. They're

supposed to give equal relocation value. Well, what's equal to the Everglades? What do they want anyhow? They already got a national park twice the size of Rhode Island. What do you have to do to appease the great God Ecology? How much of this swamp do you need?

The residents met on Mondays to discuss options and to try to find answers relating to the demise of the community. Daniel took a cardboard box from a nearby shelf and tossed it into the table's center. Throughout the week, it filled with suggestions from workers and customers about how to stop the government. Park rangers watched and listened from booths by the front window, having come for breakfast, but also for another feeding, unbeknownst to them. People with livelihoods at stake in the Big Cypress disliked the National Park Service. The new rangers, branding guns and filled with a mission of dominance of land rather than assistance with nature, put the people on edge. Like a mother defending her children from danger, the people in Ochopee desired to protect their families.

Some were defeated in courts, forced out of their homes, or run out of business. Ken and Forrest continued to battle in court while Raymond found himself forbidden from building on his own land. Daniel pondered the future of a motel and restaurant absent of all of his customers, workers, and friends. So then the rumor table came to be: a place where the people shared their grief and gained counseling. The New York reporters recorded quotes from the table:

"The feds are using dirty tactics to get landowners to sell," said one customer.

"The government is sending around the health department to tell people their wells are contaminated," said another.

"Gas stations and restaurants are getting citations for supposed *violations* that no one even winked at five years ago," said Daniel, having witnessed bogus tickets aimed at shutting down his business.

"I never knew about the all-pervasiveness of government until I got involved in the Big Cypress fight. We got agencies coming out of our ears down here. I never knew they had so many agencies. It's all harassment. If they don't get you coming they get you going. They've a million ways to crush you," said George.

The heated voices broke into yells, disgust, anguish, and frustration. Forrest grabbed the box, pulled out a slip of paper, and read a suggestion: "Bring in a herd of elephants to stomp the swamp flat." Forrest mentioned about a circus where they might get some elephants, and they laughed together about the idea. The rangers continued to listen, and at one point, when the bitter rumor makers engaged the government men, they shot back at them and said, "We're going to take everyone out of the Everglades except the Golden Lion and leave it here, just to punish you." Daniel did not see humor in the joke because he knew the reality behind it. The rumor makers held tight to their defeatist attitude and continued to share ways to destroy the Everglades behind them.

Frances grabbed a note from the box and read, "Get Happy Harry to spread melaleuca seeds in the Everglades from his plane."

Harold Enquist owned businesses in the area and often flew tourists in his plane or drove them in his taxi. They all knew of the plant and the story of how the governor of Florida in 1904, Napoleon Bonaparte Broward, envisioned draining the Everglades to make it useful for development. Melaleuca possessed the ability to absorb any surrounding water like a sponge, and once its roots gained hold, not much stopped it from prospering everywhere it touched. The government battled the nonnative species since the turn of the century and never stopped fighting. This first feasible plan pleased the round table, and all of a sudden they, felt empowerment.

"The only real way to kill them is to cover them with concrete," said Daniel. The rangers sitting in the coffee shop that day did not like to hear this plan. Referring to the National Park Service, the ranger told Daniel, with no joking in his voice, "Wait and see what they got in store for you."

WHICHELLO

1974. The government drew an imaginary line. Any developed land owned before a specific date they proclaimed grandfathered, and so the law of condemnation did not apply, but any properties attained after that date became fair game. Officials offered a sum of money. Unsatisfied customers took their case to court, where a judge determined the price.

1977. After Daniel initiated the selling of his house to the government, they declined to give him a status on the purchase of his business as he expected. He became worried that he might end up raising his family in a motel room. Daniel's tax accountant and friend, John Soldavini, had an office in Naples and so the two set up a spare room with type-writers and a hand-crank copy machine. They embarked on a campaign of letter writing. To those they knew had no interest in helping them, they sent notice of their anger and disagreement. To some, they sent a request for help, and to a few, they discussed the option of offering the Golden Lion to be included in the acquisition. The Naples office churned out letters through the month of June and into July.

Daniel opened a response from the State of Florida, Division of Recreation of Parks, dated July 15, 1977, from David J. Buchanan, Environmental Specialist, Bureau of Land Acquisition and Development. He wrote on behalf of Ney Landrum, his Director:

> Thank you for your letter of June 24, 1977, in which you express strong opposition to the acquisition of lands within the Big Cypress National Preserve. The acquisition will be the responsibility of the federal government. Therefore, we are forwarding your complaint to the National Park Service for their consideration.

A few days later, another letter arrived from Buchanan. He wrote:

> If you have not already contacted the National Park Service,
> you might consider sharing your comments directly with them.
> That agency has the responsibility of acquiring the Big Cypress
> National Preserve lands.

Three days later, a letter arrived from James F. Sewell, Land Acquisition Officer. Daniel and John read the letter, which said nothing more than Sewell tried to contact them by phone with no success and wanted to discuss the many problems mentioned in the letters.

August began, and letter responses came to the Naples office. Bill Gunter, state treasurer and insurance commissioner, wrote and suggested that Daniel have his property appraised by either writing to or visiting the Big Cypress Acquisition office in Naples where Sewell worked. He expressed that this action would cause the pace of the process to quicken. A couple days after the letter from Gunter, another letter from James Sewell showed up in the mail. Again, Sewell expressed his inability to reach the men by phone.

> If you wish to discuss the status of the Golden Lion Motor Inn,
> please contact me or Mr. Defendorf and arrange a meeting. I will
> be out of the office August 8th through August 18th.

The very next day, a third letter from Buchanan came to the office.

> The state is no longer expending monies within the Big Cypress
> National Preserve. You must contact and deal with the National
> Park Service in Naples regarding the acquisition of your property.
> If you desire to provide us with an objective analysis of your cir-
> cumstances, we will be glad to see if there is any way in which
> we may be of assistance. We certainly understand your concern for
> your livelihood and feel that the Park Service will do everything

possible to ensure against any unjust loss due to their purchasing
of lands in the Preserve.

Secretary of State of Florida, Bruce A. Smathers, wrote a letter dated August 8:

> Thank you for making me aware of your concern over the delay in
> acquisition of the Big Cypress Swamp lands and the uncertainty
> it has caused your business. In order to assist you in determining
> when you might expect to be contacted regarding acquisition of
> your property, I am forwarding a copy of your letter to Mr. Ney
> Landrum, Director, Florida Division of Recreations and Parks.

Also dated August 8, Gerald A. Lewis, Comptroller of the Department of
Banking and Finance of the State of Florida wrote a letter.

> I am taking the liberty of forwarding your letter to Mr. Harmon
> Shields, Executive Director of the Department of Natural
> Resources requesting that he respond to your inquiries.

Mid-August. Daniel wrote back to Sewell and expressed interest in meeting with the National Park Service. Soon after, the acquisition office contacted
Buchanan, who sent his fourth letter, dated August 12:

> It is understood that you can expect to receive a notice soon to set
> up a meeting date.

Also dated the twelfth, Harmon Shields, Executive Director, wrote a letter to
Daniel.

> Members of our staff have discussed the possible purchase of your
> property with the National Park Service and understand that
> they stand ready to sit down and discuss with you the particulars

of your situation. We appreciate your bringing to our attention your concern over the welfare of your business and feel that the National Park Service will do everything it properly can to ensure against any unjust loss as a result of the purchase of lands with the Preserve.

In a letter dated August 12 as well, Robert L. Shevin, Attorney General of Florida, wrote down some words for James Sewell and sent a copy to Daniel. The letter read:

I would appreciate it very much if you would respond to Mr. Whichello and provide whatever information you have available, sending me a copy of your response.

Shevin then wrote a new letter addressed to Daniel, and he sent a copy to Sewell.

I appreciate your making me aware of your concern and I hope we will be hearing from Mr. Sewell in the near future.

The Congress of the United States received word of the Golden Lion through Andy Ireland of the Eighth District of Florida in Washington, DC, and his return letter to Naples was dated August 15:

Many thanks for your letter regarding the impact of the acquisition of Big Cypress and your livelihood. I can appreciate your situation and I'm forwarding your letter to your Congressman, the Honorable L. A. Bafalis. I'm sure he will want to know about this.

Buchanan got word of the news reaching Congress and the secretary of state, and on that same day, August 15, went to writing a fifth letter to Daniel.

The Secretary of State has brought to our attention your letter ...
remaining lands within the Big Cypress National Preserve are
being negotiated and purchased by a federal team operating out
of Naples. Again, if you have not contacted the National Park
Service regarding the matter of your property, we strongly urge
you to do so.

Harmon Shields, Executive Director of the State of Florida of National
Resources, heard of the Golden Lion news reaching Congress and state officials. On
the same day, in a letter dated August 15, he wrote:

Since writing you last, we understand you and the National Park
Services office in Naples have been in contact and arrangements
are being made for a meeting. We feel the Park Service will be
interested in knowing of any circumstance peculiar to your situation and will deal with your fairly and properly.

The day after Shields sent his letter to the Naples CPA office, Florida governor,
Reuben O'D. Askew, sat down at his desk and drafted a letter to Daniel.

STATE OF FLORIDA

Office of the Governor

THE CAPITOL
TALLAHASSEE 32304

REUBIN O'D. ASKEW
GOVERNOR

August 16, 1977

Mr. Dan Whichello
Golden Lion Motor Inn
Post Office Box 23
Ochopee, Florida 33943

Dear Mr. Whichello:

Thank you for your letter of July 25 indicating your wish to have your property purchased as part of the Big Cypress National Preserve.

Acquisition of lands within the Big Cypress Preserve is the responsibility of the federal government. The State provided $40 million toward the acquisition, almost all of which has been spent. No further State expenditures are planned in that area.

When the federal government enacted legislation for the purchase of lands within the Preserve, provision was made for the acquisition of improved property with the consent of the owner, pursuant to Public Law 93-440. The Division of Recreation and Parks informed me that they discussed possible purchase of your property with the National Park Service and that the Park Service attempted to contact you on several occasions to discuss the particulars of your situation. If you have not already done so, please contact Mr. James Sewell, National Park Service, Post Office Box 1515, Naples, Florida 33940.

I understand the impact of this situation on your livelihood and feel sure that the National Park Service will do everything possible to assure against unjust loss as a result of the purchase of lands within the Preserve.

With kind regards,

Sincerely,

Governor

ROA/frs

Letter from the governor of Florida to Daniel Whichello

August 19, 1977, Sewell wrote:

> If it would be convenient for you to meet with me on Thursday, August 25th at 1:30 p.m., please notify me by Wednesday afternoon.

Daniel was not able to meet with Sewell on this date, and so Sewell wrote again:

> I discussed your situation with Superintendent Good. The earliest he can meet with you is on September 13th, at 1:30pm at my office. If this is agreeable with you, please notify me no later than September 7th.

September 2, a letter came from Sewell:

> Our letter of August 30th asked that you meet in my office at 1:30 p.m., on September 13th. Due to unavoidable circumstance Superintendent Good requests that the time be changed to September 16th at 1:30 p.m.

September 1977. Harlan Whichello, Daniel Whichello, John Whichello, CPA John Soldavini, and Representative Mary Ellen Hawkins met with NPS superintendent Good and James Sewell in a small but adequate temporary Naples acquisition office. Sewell kept the meeting short. He did not give answers to questions asked in the meeting by any of the attendees. His message he made abrupt, discourteous, and clear: that the National Park Service or any other government agency would not be purchasing the Golden Lion or helping the family in any way. Daniel, his father Harlan, and his brother John felt distraught and insulted by Sewell's reaction to their concerns.

Spring of the next year. Daniel started the Monday morning rumor association in the Golden Lion diner, and the National Park Service became the enemy of the community.

Throughout the 70s, Harlan and Daniel had joined with other leaders at the chamber of commerce to spend time away from their loved ones and businesses, becoming wrapped up in the red tape of a government bureaucracy in Tallahassee and Washington, DC. Tens of thousands of dollars had been raised by all manner of methods-including turkey shoots, charity events, festivals, banquets, donations, and money from their own pockets-accomplished nothing. The politicians played to pacify, while the NPS crept closer.

Golden Lion restaurant advertisement

In 1979, the challenge of keeping the doors open at the Golden Lion wore on Nancy, the eldest daughter. With her brother Daniel stuck fighting government, she spent days trying to find someone to cook, clean, serve food, maintain the plumbing, and fix the broken toilets in the bar bathroom. The interior department annihilated her work force and customer base. She opened half of the rooms to people willing to live in a motel and work a job. Some workers chose the taxi company that she hired to drive to Miami and Naples. Staff said good-bye to customers week by week, as their time came for leaving behind their Ochopee lives.

Back at home, government agents flew helicopters almost every week over Daniel and Marge's house, to the point where Marge started filming the activity with her 8 mm camera-as proof of harassment. On the business front, restaurant inspectors appeared and began giving out citations for unprecedented reasons-such as finding a bit of raw hamburger on a knife just used, and placed in the sink. A new law created at that time called "The Yo-yo Syndrome Law" went into effect, and authorities worked to use it against the Golden Lion by taking them to court with hopes to close their business. A suspicious television news report appeared on the local stations, criticizing the Golden Lion for digging up hundreds of acres of limestone south of their building. Daniel, his brothers, and his sisters ran a motel, a restaurant, and a bar-not a mining operation.

The message repeated to the people through hearings, in the media, and in legislation for the Big Cypress purchase was protection of water, yet the NPS bulldozed lines of homes into the canals contaminating the water. Talking with locals in the bar and restaurant, Daniel learned that some of the residents received five times the value for their smaller pieces of land. He continued to try to have government buy the Golden Lion, but they refused to even give him an offer. He read from the GAO report:

> The Land and Water Conservation Fund have fostered equally rapid increases in appropriations. At the same time Congress has also authorized a major expansion of the National Park System and granted wider general authority for Federal land purchases to other resource management agencies. In some cases, dollars have piled up faster than these agencies can spend them properly. This

in turn has resulted in some land acquisition proposals that were hastily conceived, perhaps more to utilize available funding than to address actual program needs.

This document proved to him that the government possessed the money to buy his business, even when they kept telling him that they ran out of money. So at the end of 1979, he wrote one final letter to a congressman, whom he trusted and admired, Skip Bafalis.

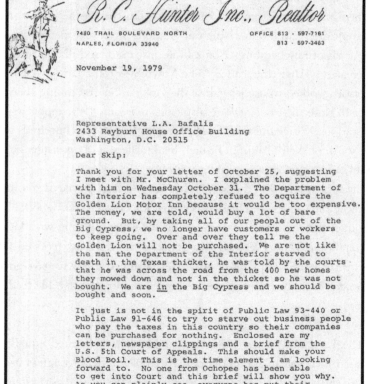

R. C. Hunter Inc., Realtor

7480 TRAIL BOULEVARD NORTH
NAPLES, FLORIDA 33940

OFFICE 813 - 597-7161
813 - 597-3463

November 19, 1979

Representative L.A. Bafalis
2433 Rayburn House Office Building
Washington, D.C. 20515

Dear Skip:

Thank you for your letter of October 25, suggesting I meet with Mr. McChuren. I explained the problem with him on Wednesday October 31. The Department of the Interior has completely refused to acquire the Golden Lion Motor Inn because it would be too expensive. The money, we are told, would buy a lot of bare ground. But, by taking all of our people out of the Big Cypress, we no longer have customers or workers to keep going. Over and over they tell me the Golden Lion will not be purchased. We are not like the man the Department of the Interior starved to death in the Texas thicket, he was told by the courts that he was across the road from the 400 new homes they mowed down and not in the thicket so he was not bought. We are in the Big Cypress and we should be bought and soon.

It just is not in the spirit of Public Law 93-440 or Public Law 91-646 to try to starve out business people who pay the taxes in this country so their companies can be purchased for nothing. Enclosed are my letters, newspaper clippings and a brief from the U.S. 5th Court of Appeals. This should make your Blood Boil. This is the time element I am looking forward to. No one from Ochopee has been able to get into Court and this brief will show you why. As you can plainly see, everyone has put their faith in the fair play the Department of the Interior would display toward the persons to be taken. Nothing can be further from the truth. The U.S. General Accounting Office just completed 8 months on its investigation and looked into 8 parks. You should read it if you get a chance.

```
                        Page 2



    The Department has sent U.S. Marshals three times
    to serve condemation papers on my home.  I have
    now been appraised and am waiting for the
    apprasial to be shown to us.

    I hope this is what you need to help us.  I have
    waited to answer you untill after the convention
    in Orlando because I knew you were busy with the
    Crane campaign.  Saw you there.  I had a very good
    time, met a lot of the candidates.

    Thank you for writing.

    Sincerely,



    Dan Whichello
    R.C. Hunter, Inc. Realtor

    DW:mac
```

Public Law 91-646: 1/2/1971

Act to provide uniform and equitable treatment of persons displaced from their homes, businesses, or farms by Federal and federally assisted programs and to establish uniform and equitable land acquisition policies for Federal and federally assisted programs.

Public Law 93-440: 10/11/1974

Act establishing the Big Cypress National Preserve and for other purposes.

Harlan Whichello's children (three boys and three girls) held high hopes for their lives in 1970 at the opening of the Golden Lion Motor Inn. They were filled with the youth of their twenties and the excitement of the adventure. In 1982, they wanted nothing but to sell the motel-restaurant. They paid hell trying to keep it running, with the primary cause being the land acquisition of the government. Daniel signed up to receive newsletters from a new grassroots organization with the desire to help protect people from government abuse: the National Park Inholders Association. Through the stories he learned that he was not alone, and then he put the issues in a box and saved them.

The family received no help from the politicians or agencies that came to take the community, and they received nothing for the business. They lost everything.

After sitting vacant for a year or so, The Golden Lion Motor Inn went up for sale at a sheriff's auction. When an environmental group bid on the property, the auctioneer stopped the bidding and let them purchase. Any further bids by private individuals were refused. The environmentalists then took the property and handed it over to the National Park Service for their Big Cypress headquarters.

Plaque screwed to the side of the Golden Lion building

"The 1986 acquisition of this Big Cypress National Preserve facility was made possible through the assistance of the National Parks and Conservation Association"

The Golden Lion Motor Inn, vacant, waiting for auction

WATSON

1976. America celebrated its bicentennial, an acknowledgement of two hundred years since the signing of the Declaration of Independence and its support of individual freedoms protected by the government, thought to be seldom found in other countries. Many Ochopee residents felt somewhat at odds with the concept, considering their situation.

Since the four square mile heart of Ochopee lost its battle to remain out of the acquisition, land official James Sewell set his sights on four hundred acres owned by Ochopee Rock Co., six hundred acres owned by Forrest Harmon, the L.P. gas plant, the concrete plant, and Watson's grocery store. In April, he began working with an appraisal firm contracted out of Miami. Since the Department of Natural Resources only employed three people to complete the paperwork for preserve purchases, they became overwhelmed by a thousand new cases. In order for a landowner to receive funds for a property, the sale required the meeting of state regulations and required approval by the governor and his cabinet. Sewell simplified the process by creating his own certificates, which declared that a purchase met the regulations. He then forwarded them to Tallahassee for signatures. The average large property took two to three months from appraisal to sale.

"I'm sick of talk about the acquisition. They could leave the people alone that already are here. They could purchase the undeveloped land and leave the people here who already are here," said Frances Watson, speaking with a visiting newspaper reporter.

On her last day as owner of the store, August 25, 1976, she bagged groceries. Kids came and went, asking for candy while Frances reflected on her life. She showed the reporter a big set of shears and explained about how she used it to clip off the shirt tails of hunters. They would walk into the store looking for supplies, talking to each other about the giant deer they almost shot but missed. Frances insisted that she chop off the bottom of their shirt, after which, she wrote on the piece, the person's name, the size of supposed animal, and how close the hunter came to hitting it. She pointed to the various pieces of shirts tacked up on the side of the wall. When the topic of her famous insulting of customers came up in the conversation, she told the reporter, "With these customers, I don't let them out of the store without giving them hell, they know I like everybody, and I don't give a damn." She pointed to a plaque hanging near the entrance that read, *Ochopee God Mother*, given to her by some local residents.

Frances left store ownership that year and spent some of her free time undergoing necessary medical operations. Across the canal from the store, she rested in her home and pondered life. The house she built with her own hands endured the weather and the wild. It hosted nights of poker games, food, and companionship, becoming a retreat for Ochopee's business leaders. Her family lived off of the land, eating the crabs and fish from the rivers, and making pies and wine from the numerous orange, grape fruit, plum, fig, lemon, mango, kumquat, and key lime trees.

In the late sixties, her eight-year-old daughter, Joann, saw a twelve-foot alligator come up to the house. The women called park rangers to help them, but they refused. Natives from their Seminole village then arrived and took the gator to a new location.

As an adult, Joann learned of oil discoveries in Big Cypress. On a day not long after, she and her mother watched through a window at the front of their house, looking at many large, four-door white pickup trucks with Texas plates, driving in and out of the area. Days later, government men visited Frances and all of her neighbors, wishing to acquire each and every property. Some stubborn trailer owners agreed on sale prices three times the value of their property before moving, and so the Watsons watched as their neighborhood shrunk. With no interest in selling, and not having to because of the age of the house, Frances carried on as usual.

The following year, Frances and Joann spotted government workers blocking up parts of the canal that ran near their home. They filled in culverts used to drain water, with dirt, and then left. In the next months, the summer rains poured down on the home where Frances lay sick from another operation, this time on her gallbladder. For the first time, since building the house in the early 1950s, the water rose up to the front door, went inside, and filled every room. It kept coming, bringing with it plant matter and fish. When the water finished, it remained at a constant six inches in depth. Frances lay in pain with minnows swimming around her chair. After weeks of draining, she was left with a ruined house, no way to rebuild it, and no money to pay for it. Then government men working with the acquisition came to see her again, and they offered a small sum of money for the property. With no other option, she took the money and moved to Immokalee.

In 1991, Joann Watson returned to the home of her childhood. She hoped to find something of her past to take with her-a piece of the house even. The father of her children, David, followed her across the old wooden bridge that traversed the canal, leading to the Watson place. She looked for the fruit trees that she ate from for so many years, but the park service bulldozed and burned them all, declaring them a nonnative species. She found nothing of the house, destroyed as well. Farther into the woods, a trail led to rock pits, where she and her neighbors used to swim in the summers. She hoped to go visit and reminisce about her simple Ochopee life. A park ranger stopped his vehicle on the side of the road and walked across the bridge to confront the unknown people. He asked to know their business, and when Joann told him a little of her life and the reason for their trip, he said, "You are trespassing, and you shouldn't be trespassing here." He emitted an attitude of arrogance, and he made sure that the two saw the gun holstered on his leg. He did not allow them to go see the rock pits, and so they left.

HARMON

"Tell me where you can buy a place anywhere in the world with this kind of climate for $450 or five hundred dollars an acre. Much of it is swamp, but just as much is usable farmland that once was the tomato-growing capital of the world," Forrest Harmon told a newspaper reporter. He explained that a price of $1,500 was the average cost that the government had paid to other landowners across the country. Here in Ochopee, people paid $3,000 an acre when they had first bought their land, and now the government offered just three hundred dollars. Forrest refused to pay the low-ball offer, and he joined other people in a law-suit against the government. He faced a judge after waiting three years to go to court. All cases without representation, the government processed first, so those with lawyers waited and waited. He and his wife, Donna, came together with their lawyer, Toby Prince Brigham. Toby handled a hundred of the cases in the Big Cypress. The three stood listening to Judge Merkins.

"You'd have to have hip boots and a compass to even find your property," said the judge. Forrest turned to his lawyer and asked if they could get a different judge. The request angered Merkins. When Forrest took the stand to testify, Merkins proceeded to cross-examine him, a process not legal by a judge. He then ordered a charge of perjury against Forrest.

Forrest submitted an appeal, and the court granted him a different judge. The case continued. The new arbitrator told Forrest that he was not allowed to develop his land any further, although he was given the option to put a trailer park on his property. Forrest knew that doing that would only devalue the land so that the government could ask for a lower price. After four months-that included twenty–nine days of testimony to figure out the land's value-the judge offered Harmon another impossible price for his hundreds of acres of land, home, trailer parks, and Rock

Company. The Harmons refused and went on to 11th US Circuit Court of Appeals. The three-judge panel then upheld the award and method of determining the value. The Harmon family lost their entire life's accomplishments on the swing of a gavel.

Ochopee, Midge Lessor

> *The loss of Harmon and the Golden Lion has ruined our community. Life has never been the same. If you were lonely and needed a shoulder to lean on, head for the lion in the Everglades; that's how I met Forrest. I visited him in the nursing home until he left for heaven.*

In 2014, seventyish Midge continued to live in her house that she built with her husband on almost two-hundred acres of swampland where she defended her chickens from bears with a shot gun. She made her living raising cows, horses, and exotic Persian cats.

Forrest helped build the Chamber of Commerce building a few years after he arrived in Ochopee. The right side of the building hosted many turkey shoots for the community. Ochopee and Everglades City leaders met here over the decades to discuss business and at one point, ways to save Ochopee and fight the government takeover. This picture was taken in 2013, and the building is rumored to become obsolete. The NPS owns the land under the structure-*future causality?*

GAUNT'S POST OFFICE

Hardworking and resilient to adversity, James Gaunt fought the mosquitoes, animal dangers, fires, and flooding. He envisioned something from nothing. The first to import labor into Collier County, he created jobs for the natives, blacks, and whites alike. He cared about his workers by providing for their needs and wants to the best of his ability. Those who knew him well called him Jimmy and described him as "a prince of a man" and "the nicest guy." From a world new to the modern miracle of electricity, Gaunt embraced the invisible force. Its potential excited him.

Well into the Ochopee project, he pursued rural electrification to advance business and farming for all of South Florida. Soon after the infamous act of using an irrigation shed for the post office, he joined the board overseeing the regional electric company, called the Lee county electric Cooperative. From 1953 to 1956 he was vice president, and then he served as president from 1956 to 1981. In 1957, he was the official Ochopee and Everglades City representative. Later in life, he put his full efforts into getting an agriculture research center in Immokalee. A generous and charitable man, he brought the Lion's Club to Ochopee and carried the role of president for the Collier County division. The Lion's Club organization took up the work of Helen Keller after her speech in 1925. An Alabama native struck blind and deaf before two years of age, Helen spent her adult life crusading for relief for victims of disabilities. In his retirement at age seventy-two in 1972, Gaunt led meetings at the Golden Lion Motor Inn, a location with a fitting name. There he met and developed a friendship with owner Daniel Whichello and at one point invited him to serve on the board of the cooperative. Alongside Daniel, Gaunt attended the chamber of commerce meetings for the Everglades City area. Father of Ochopee, Gaunt continued to keep his invention close and stayed active in the politics, often meeting with his good friend W. H. Turner, the Collier County manager.

By the 1970s, Ochopee belonged to many people, and Gaunt cared about them as much as his original colony. He hated to see government intrude on their rights and force the people from their land. When he attended the chamber meetings, he often donated money to help with the expenses of fighting government, which included transportation, food, and administrative and legal services. At Frances Watson's home, Jimmy sat with the residents playing poker into the Friday nights and stood beside them at the hearings during the days, while giving the politicians his mind. He blamed them for the suffering they caused to his homestead.

The local community painted the Smallest Post Office to help raise awareness for Heart Disease during the month of February 2013

*Replica of the famous post office on a float in the first and only
Everglades City Halloween parade in 1970*

SHEALY

The Shealy brothers lost touch with many friends due to the acquisition, some of which were customers. Because of the age of their development, the government did not condemn and take their land, but instead increased regulations over time. When short on food, they relied on their upbringing to hunt in the swamp.

David Shealy at the Golden Lion

With the small camp store selling supplies and the campground bringing in outdoorsmen, they managed to make it to the 1980s. Ochopee leaders knew their fate by reviewing documentation received through The Freedom of Information Act, which showed the plans of the Department of the Interior. Eyewitness, Jack Shealy, at twenty-five years of age, studied a map with Raymond Wooten.

> It's one of their most recent of many steps to destroy Everglades City; they will advertise the Big Cypress Visitor Center two miles farther east with large signs. Raymond Wooten showed me government blue-prints of what was planned for that visitor Center back in '81 or '82; that's how far they plan ahead. It showed swamp buggy rides to the north, airboat rides to the south, and canoe rentals for Halfway Creek. I saw it with my own eyes back in the early eighties. -Jack Shealy

Laws passed throughout the eighties caused the elimination of business for the Shealy family by increased hunting and fishing regulations. Most outdoorsmen stopped coming to use their camp due to shortened seasons, periodic closings and finally regulations forbidding hunting in certain parts. In 1988, with the loss of their mother and last living parent, the brothers took on full responsibility of the family business.

An amendment passed, allowing the park to buy approximately 147,000 acres, called the *addition lands*, and to ban swamp buggies. This legislation killed the interest for hunters. Jack and David struggled for the coming years. At one low point, Jack sat at a picnic table and made key chains out of empty blue crab claws, using cement and a metal eye hole for the key ring. At $4.95 each, he sold enough to pay the electric bill. Later, laws forbid the removal of anything from the land, such as empty crab claws, so he was not allowed to sell the key chains.

The brothers realized that they needed to do something, or face homelessness. With the opening of an animal sanctuary, they attracted attention from some media and from family visitors with children wanting to learn about nature. A good friend and animal expert named Rick worked on-site teaching children and their parents about alligators, snakes, birds, turtles, and plant species growing in his garden.

In the mid-1990s, David sat outside of his camp store watching cars passing by on US 41, and wondered about his future. Every day he fought to keep what little was left of his father's vision. He decided not to be beaten. For most of his life he studied, researched, and learned about the strange sight that he witnessed in childhood. He loved the stories of the Skunk Ape creature, and so he invented the Skunk Ape Research Center. After unraveling and posting a large canvas sign across the camp store, he then wrote a field manual, made a video documentary complete with music sound track, ordered cups, t-shirts, hats, bumper stickers, lighters, and key chains advertising this mysterious wonder.

Word went out to the media, and after years of hard work of campaigning, educating, and performing local radio and television interviews, David found himself succeeding. Prominent radio station host Todd Schnitt aka M.J. Kelli of 93.3 FLZ, treated him to a hotel room and broadcast time in Tampa Bay. Soon, other media outlets contacted the Skunk Ape Hunter. David revealed his story to the Travel Channel, The Learning Channel, *Unsolved Mysteries*, *National Geographic*, *Reader's Digest*, *Roadside America*, *Florida Living*, and other magazines. A large German population toured the Everglades, and many stopped to learn at the Shealys' wilderness center. International attention landed him an interview with the Florida International University and an environmental documentary called *"My America"* that aired across many countries in Europe.

January 1999. The Florida Department of Transportation recognized a fifty mile segment of US 41 East as a Florida Scenic Highway. The section of road ran in front of the Shealy campground and was the second highway in the state to have the designation. Representatives from the National Park Service, the US Fish and Wildlife Service, the Florida Department of Environmental protection, and the Florida Department of Transportation led public planning officials and some private citizens for two years to gain control over the road. Named Corridor Advisory Group or CAG, these people who did not reside off of this road, had at their disposal hundreds of thousands of dollars from the state government to alter it for their personal preference. Gene Casey, a representative of the organization, visited David concerning his sign and replica of the Skunk Ape which he used to draw business. The group's intention appeared to desire the removal of David's advertisements.

The next year, additional park service representatives along with the U.S. Department of Transportation's Federal Highway Administration members formed a federal group called Corridor Management Entity or CME to acquire additional say so over US 41. They honored the road with a designation called "National Scenic Byway" and received grant money from a twenty five million dollar bucket.

Government grants were given for various projects such as beautification of the sides of a road or the building of bike passages. These federal transportation programs provided an outside organization decision-making power over land around local people already living in the vicinity. The results sometimes affected these people without their knowledge, and in some cases, they found themselves in a situation too late to act or interject their opinions. The Shealys and their neighbors witnessed a progressive pattern of control over the trail by people other than themselves, beginning with the Big Cypress legislation in 1974. In another designation in the country, the committees cleared buildings and hid businesses from the view of passing customers. This possibility upset the Shealy brothers.

While word of the Skunk Ape grew through the 2000s, also did legislation. In 2000, a completed off-road vehicle plan stated that the area around Jack and David, known as *"zone one"* or the *"Stair Steps Unit"* once passed, prevented the brothers from being able to ever use their off-road vehicles in the land around their home to hunt. This ban led to a major reduction in campground attendance of hunters and ORV enthusiasts.

Further rules removed all motorized vehicles from the swamp and left the family with only boats that they could push or paddle with a stick. Promoting the Skunk Ape became more important than ever since it represented one of the last methods they possessed to make a living.

In the next few years, Ochopee and Everglades City feared changes made by outsiders as the CME group began making plans for US 41 involving raising the road in certain spots and creating bike trails and animal crossings. Backed by the Florida Department of Transportation, an environmental group known as The Defenders of Wildlife pushed into being a ten-foot tall fence which ran for miles along SR 29. It was designed to keep panthers from crossing the highway, but the angled barbed-wire snared panthers and linkage caused deer to get their antlers stuck in the fence.

Mid-2005. The Collier County Metropolitan Planning Organization composed mainly of Collier County Citizens felt that people not living in the area held too much power over their county, and that the designations were created illegally. They then voted to remove both the state and federal designations-the first time in the history for any road.

> An MPO is a federally mandated and federally funded transportation policy-making organization in the United States and is made up of representatives from local governing bodies and public transportation authorities.
> -Collier MPO website

In March of 2007, a group of people joined together and created the Sportsman's Alliance. Chairman of the Collier County Commission Jim Coletta attended and supported the movement, which helped to fight intrusion of public liberty in the Big Cypress. Some of the National Park Service officials became angry over this action.

In 2008 the NPS began building a multi-million dollar visitor center in Ochopee similar to the one Jack saw in the plans. It was placed a few miles from the Shealy campground and next to the old Golden Lion Building-NPS Big Cypress headquarters. Also that year, the Park Service assisted the Department of Transportation with the further desires of The Defenders of Wildlife. The group wished to build another fence along US 41 which by design, closed off the Shealy's property from the Everglades. The structure threatened to wall them inside, making them prisoners on their own land-in essence hostages. This action would also contribute to the end of their opportunities for hunting and squash their last few freedoms. The parties involved looked to construct panther road crossings at the spot just east of the camp. The brothers feared that the raised road might block their campground from the view of Miami traffic causing the loss of customers.

The proposed fence affected the Native Americans living alongside the road as well. Natives, gladesmen, elders from Everglades City, and some wise people formed together to fight. From a letter written to the Superintendent Pedro Ramos of the Big Cypress National Preserve in 2008 by a Tribal Chairman:

> This is blatant single-species management, which has been proven time and time again to not work and have dire consequences for other species. The proposed fence would bar other animals from access to the canal. How would deer, raccoons, opossums, otters, gators, turtles, and other species gain access to the canal? Gators and turtles would hit the fence and keep trying to get through rather than find some other way around. Other animals would suffer at the expense of trying to protect one species.
>
> The tribe does not want US 41 to look like SR 29. These wildlife fences are bad for tourism; they destroy scenic vistas, and would make US 41 appear like a prison or an equipment yard.

From a letter written in 2009 by the threatened Native tribe to the Fish and Wildlife Service, the superintendent of the Big Cypress National Park Service, and to Elizabeth Fleming, the responsible party at the Defenders of Wildlife for panther protection:

Statement of Aboriginal People of Florida

We only just found out about the planning of a project to put wildlife crossings and fencing located at US 41 at Turner River in Big Cypress National Preserve. Aboriginal people didn't just come here overnight. We have been living our way of life in our own land from generation to generation since the beginning of creation.

Big Cypress National Preserve was illegally established on Aboriginal land, so we do not have a right to say what should or should not happen at Big Cypress National Preserve because Big Cypress National Preserve is illegally on our land.

We do not agree with the planning of the proposed project to put wildlife crossings and fencing located at US 41 at Turner River. We want you to stop the planning process of this project. You never asked us about this project and this project lies within an area of Big Cypress National Preserve.

The plan of the Aboriginal People is: God gave them their rights to take care of all his Creation. So we do have a right to do that. God gave us a law to follow and that is the law we follow.

After many letters, phone calls, and discussions, the government and the environmental group decided not to pursue the fence and road-crossing plan. All parties dropped the issue and the natives and the Shealy brothers went back to trying to raise their families and live their lives in peace.

In the next couple years, the NPS took work trucks down the road east of the Shealys' place and upgraded their remote campgrounds which they had made at an earlier time. Since these campgrounds were at no cost to the public they contributed to loss of income for Jack and David as they could not compete with free.

David Shealy, the Skunk Ape Hunter and survivor

WOOTEN

First a farmer then a mechanic and a finally boat builder, Raymond pushed the limits of his abilities. Decades of living in the Everglades taught him to appreciate nature but also to maintain it. When authorities forbid the hunting of alligators due to their critical population levels in Florida, he used his firsthand expertise to help repopulate the species. Raymond, the biologist and embryologist stepped onto the scene. In a trailer on his property, he set up a successful incubation laboratory that kept alligator eggs in an environment similar to their nest in the wild. Hatched babies were safe from natural predators, and once they matured, protected from hunters. Towering steel fences enclosed hundreds of gators on the farm behind the airboat business. So successful with his endeavor, Raymond gained notoriety and respect from fellow biologists and government scientists across Florida and the nation. Raymond's sanctuary grew into a sort of animal park.

On the property, he used a dragline to create a large pond for dolphins, Lady and Dolly, and then spent a year training the two to do tricks for patrons in a show. Around the back of the gift shop, the extended family pets swam to a dock, where Raymond stood wielding a steel rod, which he spun in a circular motion. Around his waist, a guard kept him from falling into the water, and then he leaned forward, giving the porpoises the signal to swim backward. After completing such tasks, he rewarded them with pieces of fish.

Raymond Wooten and his dolphins

Raymond also set land aside for some deer and enclosures for crocodiles, snakes, turtles, raccoons, otters, bobcats, a couple of Florida panthers, and a black spotted panther. Visitors came to see the animals at close quarters, and the staff taught them about each one.

North of US 41, the terrain became a dry highland known as the Cypress swamp, where deer and panthers roamed among the alligators. He wanted to educate people on the entire area, so he invested in a swamp buggy business. Bodiless, roofless trucks on six-foot tall tractor wheels kept people high off of the ground and gave them a panoramic view. These machines let onlookers take in the natural beauty at their leisure. Airboats took passengers through the watery south side; swamp buggies took them into the muddy north; and in between, the animal sanctuary completed the experience. More than just famous, word of the Wooten's airboat and swamp buggy adventure spanned the globe.

One of the Wooten's early swamp buggies

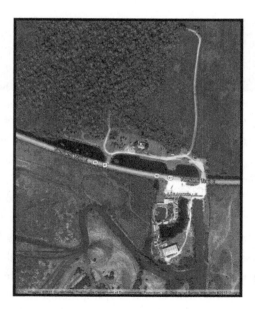

Google map of Wooten's land, showing the swamp buggy track to the north and the dolphin pond in the south

In the seventies, Raymond's family grew large, with plenty of children. They gathered around the dinner table each night after a long day helping with the family business or after church on Sundays.

Everyone kept busy with enough work to go around and plenty of people willing to help, but when US President Nixon announced the takeover of the Everglades, Raymond worried. He attended the 1971 Golden Lion meeting concerning a hearing in Miami, and as the years passed, he became more involved. Fear for their livelihoods was the main topic at the chamber of commerce meetings, where Forrest Harmon led the charge to raise money. Raymond stepped down as leader after spending eight years guiding them. President and owner of the Golden Lion, Daniel Whichello, took the position in the early 1970s.

Because the family grew, Raymond needed to build a house for him and his wife. He also wanted a special building to work with fiberglass for boats. New regulations enacted by the planning committee, headed up by Robert Rhodes, said that he now must ask them before he built anything new on his own land. In the past, he designed his world to his liking, with no issue. The unknown group of men in Tallahassee, far at the other end of the state, began to dictate his life. Raymond applied for permission to build his house. The planning committee told him no. He reapplied, and they told him no again. A once-happy man with a prosperous future, Raymond Wooten felt frustrated and angry, and these feelings forced him further into the fight between the people of Ochopee and their government. He went with the other leaders to Tallahassee and Washington, DC, to talk to senators and representatives. The clock ticked; Raymond tried to play the game, but the government refused to grant him the special permission. Determined not to be bossed around by bureaucratic strangers, he gathered his tools, drew out a blueprint, bought all of the necessary supplies, and built his building. Still new to their powers and possessing limited enforcement ability, the planners themselves did not pursue him in a direct manner.

Daniel often visited Raymond at his business. The two chatted one day outside in the heat while Raymond operated a drag-line, digging in the mud to make room for his boats to launch. A van pulled into the parking lot, and a group of people with camera equipment jumped out. The mob ran over to the two Ochopee men, and commenced angry shouting. Raymond shut down the machine, looked up from the water at them, and yelled, "Hold on, wait." He climbed up the bank, brushed the dirt from his pants, took his ball cap from his head and held it on his arm in a respectful pose. He approached the men, smiled, and said, "OK, I'm ready." They then threatened with lawsuits and heated words denouncing the airboat business and its destruction of the Everglades, the animals, and nature. Daniel and Raymond tried to make sense of it all.

Through the 1980s, government agencies enacted a host of rules and regulations. Laws banned the use of airboats in the ten thousand islands, and also on the land right up to the edge of Raymond's property line. His airboat trips took passengers on amazing expeditions into those islands, but with the regulations, they became confined to just thirty acres. The experience changed forever. Another regulation passed, outlawing digging in the swamp, which prevented airboats from running during the dry season. Additional rules on mangrove plants forbid anyone from moving them or clearing a few away to make a path for an airboat, though mangroves massed across South Florida with an abundant quantity. Later rules controlled the size of billboards, and thus, only chance motorists noticed them. A variety of permit and license requirements, bonds, USDA regulations, and ordered land surveys that cost in the tens of thousands all worked to nickel and dime Wooten's airboats.

Built before the government's *line in the swamp*, Raymond's land did not fall victim to direct eminent domain. The Department of the Interior could not condemn the property and take it, so they waited on regulation, while the Wooten family struggled.

Raymond's eldest son, Richard, had a daughter, Kim, who grew up with the appreciation of alligators. Her grandfather taught her not to fear the nature in the Everglades. He showed her how to pick up the babies and take care of them to preserve their species.

On the higher ground of the north side of US 41, next to the swamp buggy operation, sat three residential trailers. Richard, his wife, and their daughter Kim stayed in one, while Raymond and his wife stayed in another. The third belonged to his second eldest son, Willard and his wife. Raymond kept free-roaming alligators on the property and one large one that lived in the pond behind the trailers. He made sure that they were always fed; in this way, they became less of a danger. Kim asked him once why he didn't enclose these animals, and he told her that buggy riders liked to see them in their natural habitat.

Once, a family of manatees came into the inlet near the trailers, and Kim fed the mother, father, and baby by hand with heads of lettuce. She gathered her school books in the mornings and waited at the mailbox for the bus to arrive. When the children on the bus saw her standing, they sometimes also saw the one big alligator from the pond. On Friday afternoons, she met her grandmother who sat in a chair attached to an airboat, floating near the bank. Kim jumped into the front of the boat and seated herself. After its engine roared to life the child and her grandmother headed into the wild. At Raymond's hunting camp, Kim picked guavas and fished while her grandfather and his sons hunted frogs.

> Behind our trailer was a pond where I would sometimes go fishing and had to always be on the lookout for the large gator that lived there. Sometimes at night, you could hear the cries of raccoons knowing one had fallen into the pond and would soon be dinner for that lucky gator. That gator also liked to relocate at night from the back pond to the front canal; I could always see the tracks in the sand the next day. Every morning, sitting next to our mailbox, was that "special gator," lying on the bank, collecting the sunshine. For most people that would have been a scary situation; for me, it was only natural to have a gator keep me company while I waited on my school bus every morning.
> -Kimberly Wooten

By 1992, Raymond and his son Willard had passed away, and his eldest, Richard, left the business due to health issues. The youngest, Gene, and Raymond's wife, Lillian, did their best to continue. Competition from Everglades City businesses-not tied down to the government rules-lured the Wootens' customers, reducing income needed to maintain boats. At one desperate point, workers agreed to drive the airboats for only tips, since the business did not generate enough income to pay them.

In 2011, the land went up for sale, and in the middle of 2013, a competing company bought the property. After sixty years of friendships, hard work, and love for family, Wooten's Airboats ended, and a new chapter began under a young and inspired family. With hope for the future, the Wootens' name would continue, preserved by the Patel family.

For decades, Raymond and his sons built many boats by hand, and a few of them they designated as special racing crafts. His family team attended events across South Florida, competing against other airboat enthusiasts, but the Wooten team continued to outmatch and dominate its competition. This accomplishment added to the many for Raymond and his legacy.

Raymond Wooten, winning one of his great races

Airboats today:

The National Park's general management plan for the next 15 to 20 years called for an end to all private airboating in the East Everglades. The 60-year-old president of the airboat association said in an interview about limiting access to the area:

> This place is special. I have pictures of my daughter climbing the trees. My daughter is 40 now and still climbs the trees. They will put up markers and boundaries and tell us we can't go there because it's virgin land. There's something that's been here longer than the park's been here and that's Gladesmen culture. We don't want to destroy something we want to share with our children and grandchildren. We're just trying to hang onto our rights.

Some believed that the taking of the airboats from the people was because of money as Erwin, secretary of the airboat club said:

> You ate whatever you found out there. You'd stick a couple frogs, kill a deer. Anything the park does, they kick out the people who truly love it and let in snowbirds. You get on your little boardwalk and take pictures. With the park service, it's all about parks for profit.

WEIMER

When the government condemned Ken and Jeanie Weimer's home and business acreage and then offered them a fraction of the value, Ken told them, *"Hell no."* Surrendering his life's work, to Ken, was like giving up his life. He attained a lawyer and went to court. The Weimers worked their way through the system for five years, using appeals, until reaching the Florida Supreme Court. While sitting at trial, Jeanie's thoughts turned toward Ochopee, and she wished how much she would rather be home-in her sanctuary. She hoped for the finishing of the dreadful court case.

She couldn't figure out what they did so wrong. They kept being told about some watershed, but she didn't understand because ever since Ken lived in the Everglades, there had been no problems with any water. He had been there more than half of his life. Everything that was Ken was in Ochopee. A good man, he did not deserve to be treated in this way, and so she thought that she could have not hated anything more than her abusive ex-husband, who beat and controlled her. When she saw how Ken was treated by the government representatives and their policies, she realized that something worse did exist. At one time, she felt respect for her government, but now it seemed impossible. The word she used to describe their treatment: *cruel.*

In the finale of the long fight, the judge awarded them a small portion of the value of the over four-hundred acres of prime farmland, all of the water company and buildings, two housing developments, and the worst cost: the ability to make a living, his retirement, the dream he sought to pass on to his children, and his pride. He felt robbed. As for the house, the government ordered such a low value for the property that Ken's lawyer managed a deal so that the couple might stay in it for a few more years, but in the end received no compensation for the house. After saying good-bye to their way of life, they took the given amount and bought a peanut farm in Alabama.

For years after, Ken was so bitter that he would not even discuss the incident. He loved the Everglades and never stopped thinking about that life, and he asked for his wife to take his ashes back to where he considered his real home. When he died, she drove from Alabama to Ochopee and scattered them into the water behind their house.

Their daughter left her next, and so Jeanie drove again to place her ashes in the water at the same location. She then started a tradition. Each year, she traveled to the house and sat on the bank of the canal and spent time talking to her family.

By 2009, at the age of eighty-three, having suffered a stroke the year before, she no longer could drive, so she asked a friend to take her down Tamiami Trail, out to Ochopee, and passed a newly posted *"no trespassing"* sign. She sat on the dock and visited with her family, but had been there just a short time when a park ranger approached. He ordered her and the friend out of the area, and so she left.

Later that year, she passed away, and the friend, by Jeanie's request, ignored the law and released her ashes to the Everglades.

The new multi-million dollar National Park Service visitor center, opened in 2009 in a "protected water shed," at the same location where Ken Weimer built his real estate office

Daniel Whichello at Ken Weimer's real estate office in 1969

A KID IN THE SWAMP

Well, I'll say life was good out in Ochopee. We all had children about the same age. They played around and found their own entertainment. —Daisy Gaunt

1968. Dad sold his half of the Hitching Post, a trailer hitch installation and supply company, and then bought mom a house with the money. A modular building, the two pieces came by flatbed truck down US 41, past the sawgrass, the alligators, and the vultures. It turned onto a dirt road and drove a quarter of a mile south and stopped in the middle of the swamp.

The summer of 1969. Mom, age twenty-one, sat on a lawn chair in front of the house with her German shepherd by her side. She watched work-men in the distance milling about at the site of Dad's dream-project. An explosion shook the bedrock, and mom put her hand on her stomach-tight after just three months.

When her mother left to return to her husband, over a thousand miles away, Mom raised her baby alone in the little house. Dad spent days and nights working, while Mom watched the motel grow out of the horizon, brick by brick. Over the treeless plain, the only solace came from Ken Weimer's lonesome trailer and in another direction, Daniel's parents' small house.

An omnipresent silence permeated the swamp. None of the engine and siren commotion of vehicles or the clattering voices of people was present. In the first years of life, sounds played a vital influence on developing patience and a sense of peace. Mom followed through with the dutiful precision of the clock that struck eight, denoting bedtime, and was undeterred by my hand pointing at the daylight through the window. But every full, rested night led to a full day of exploration. In the backyard, Dad built a picnic table, where I sat and watched the water in the canal move. My new ears searched out ambient noises on the wind: fish jumping and splashing, crickets clicking, palm fronds rustling, and others without definition. I wandered around the house, alone, my only company, my baby sister, who lay in a bassinet. I tried to keep up with the adults.

Reprinted from the *Everglades City Mullet Rapper*, 2012:

No Fish

At age four in Ochopee, I watched my parents fish off of the bank of the canal. With this observation in mind, I took a stroll. I found a stick under a tree, a ball of string, and a pair of scissors in the kitchen drawer. After taking some washers from my dad's tool box, I slipped five of them onto the string, attached a safety pin, and then tied the string to the end of the stick. From the refrigerator, I selected bologna as bait.

The slope of the boat ramp at my grandfather's house made it easy for me to reach the water's edge. I cast the line out and watched it sink. I was surprised to see a strange, many-legged creature snatch the bologna away and then disappear. I tried again, and again it left with the bait. On my next attempt, I yanked the pole to stop the thief, but it gripped the safety pin. The pin, bait, washers, and the creature flew out of the water, over my head, and landed on the grass. The strange animal paused, and then scurried into the water. I rebaited. On the third time of flinging the odd fish onto the grass, I ran and grabbed it but suffered a harsh pinch. I let go, and off it went into the water. Determined, I fetched a bucket from the garage. When the thing was in my hands this time, I tossed it into the bucket. I showed my parents and asked if I could keep it. They said no. They took it, cooked it, and let me have a taste of the *blue crab*'s claws. After that experience I caught more of them and sometimes pulled off their claws even when they were still alive. I had become a barbarian.

Standing on the side of US 41, I wiped the sleep out of my eyes and watched the big yellow bus getting closer.

I was four-years-old, waiting alone in Everglades City, holding a rug under one arm and wearing a name badge around my neck. More people than I ever imagined circled. I wanted to go home.

Every afternoon, the bus returned me to the Everglades, and when the noise of the bus' loud motor disappeared, I breathed the quiet air. In my head roamed stories of Mit the Monkey, Mat the Rat, and Sis the snake. I pondered the odd plastic people, each making their surprise arrivals to tell us about the *letter* they represented. The swamp provided no after-school activities, such as soccer, little league, or other children-just my sister, stumbling around, trying to follow me everywhere I went.

In February of 1975, I jumped off of the last step of the bus and found the rock I had kicked from my house to the bus stop that morning. I kicked it, walked, then whacked it again, and kept going. Near the end of a canal, I passed the two familiar tall, thin palm trees placed side by side. A fat alligator lay on the bank, and so I stopped and shivered with eyes fixed on the thing that filled my nightmares. In these years, more often sight rather than sound came to the forefront of focus. I took a step, and the animal dove into the water with a huge splash. I ran the rest of the way and burst through the front door of the house, down the hall, and into the back bedroom to tell Mom what I had seen. In the middle of the queen-size bed sat something small, rolled up in a blanket. Mom entered the room, lifted the object, turned it, and then showed it to me. Its shape reminded me of a peanut. "It's your new brother," she said.

Though the population in the house grew, neither of the two new arrivals possessed the ability to satisfy my play needs. I turned to the animal life. Through increased range of sight and mobility, the world widened, and with the discovery of each new life form, I felt surprised all over again. The jiggling black specks in the early summer grew into the biggest bug in the land: grasshoppers with bright yellow legs and orange backs outlined in black. I cupped one with two hands and it stayed still as I opened them a little and stared at its strange face. I closed them again and the creature kicked with hind legs and flapped with wings. I pondered the tickling sensation, and later took one to observe by placing it in an old fish tank. The docile little pet covered the leaves I fed it with brown icky ooze, and then ate. Next to the insect, I kept some minnows, fetched from the backyard canal, and gave them all names.

Some television waves managed to reach the antenna contraption that Dad bolted to the roof. When dialing through the three channels did not result in *Speed Racer, Ben the Bear,* or *Flipper,* I headed to the yard and ran around the house or raced through the dirt on a tricycle. At the end of many days, we took dinner to the picnic table, where I ate under the dimming-blue canopy and watched the cattails down by the water, while thinking about the last book I read from the Everglades City library. Books became the greatest discovery outside of the swamp. I imagined an alternate world under the ground and pretended to try and find the doorway that reached it.

The year my brother joined us, Dad moved the family into a motel room at the Golden Lion, because he needed to sell the house for money to build a new house. To make life easier, he took a sledge-hammer to the wall between two rooms and made a doorway. In our life at the motel, my sister and I roamed the halls, peeking around corners, and moving the linen on the maids' carts while they cleaned the rooms. We climbed into one of the giant clothes bins, ran under a stairwell, or jumped through the little door that led to the roof to hide from customers. Sometimes, we fed alligators bread around back at the fishing pond. Other days, we marched through the motel lobby, took mints out of the bowl at the main desk, ordered lunch in the diner and then charged it to the establishment.

Our new house, Dad started with a basic rectangular building with a peaked roof for the attic. He realized that this design did not fit his family's space needs, but he lacked the money to build a bigger one, so he improvised. In the blueprints, he created a second floor from the attic by moving the two halves of the roof away from each other, and then he covered them with a flat top. He spread the paperwork across a table and asked me to choose on which side of the house I wanted for me and my brother's room. The room on the south end of the house lay above the parents' bedroom, so I chose the north side. My dad and his dad then went to work, flatting the foundation dirt, marking out the floor with wood, and pouring cement. After the trusses were placed along the concrete block walls, the plywood shingled, and the outer bricks sealed, Dad realized his accidental achievement. The building resembled the familiar shape of his favorite pizza restaurant, Pizza Hut, and thus the start of many jokes.

The beginning of the Pizza Hut House

Looking out of the front window of my new house

The big bedroom had a beautiful view through a wide window overlooking the Everglades. Just after being put to bed one night, I climbed out through that window, walked along the slanted roof of the house, and arrived at my sister's side. She jumped out of her pajamas when I banged on the glass.

I spent days in my bedroom coming up with an assortment of projects, based on the expanding known world. The closet became a McDonald's drive-through, complete with dessert cake-a wooden bowl turned over with toothpaste icing and cake sprinkles. On another day, the upstairs became a city with an interstate highway to my sister's room, formed with masking-tape roads complete with matchbox cars, shoe boxes for buildings, a campground, and a motel based on the Golden Lion.

Up at the real motel, the aunts, uncles, both sets of grandparents, neighbors, and friends, all worked together day after day. I sat in the bar at one of the round tables sipping on a Shirley Temple and eating the oranges and cherries that the bartender handed me. I thought of my new house, my Everglades playground, and the great family that never ceased to show their care for others. I was going on eight-years-old and felt quite satisfied.

Reprinted from the *Everglades City Mullet Rapper*, July 2012:

Bored in a Motel Room

New Year's Eve, 1977 in Ochopee, David Carradine, Kate Jackson, and members of the film crew from the movie *Thunder and Lightning* joined some members of the Miami Dolphins football team at the Golden Lion Motor Inn's New Year's Party. My mother informed me and my two-year younger, six-year-old sister that during the party we would be renting a room.

Our grandfather operated the front desk. I lifted my head to see over the counter to take the key, after which he escorted us to our room. We proceeded to watch television. Throughout the evening, Mom made calls to check on us, but we knew how to get a-hold of anyone if we needed anything; we just dialed zero. Not long after becoming bored, we dialed zero.

"Grandpa, can you bring us some ice cream?" Grandpa responded to the room with two heaping sundaes. The ice cream was eaten, and we were tired of television. I pulled out all of the drawers from the dresser, and I found a Gideon's bible. Flipping through the pages, we took turns reading aloud until we were bored. We turned to our television. A commercial came on for Pepsi, and the announcer told us to call five random people and ask them if they liked Pepsi or Coke. I grabbed the phone book and my sister and I shared dialing the rotary phone, taking down the answers as we called the public. It turned out that Pepsi won. Our television, we believed, would never lie to us, but now we were looking around for something else to do.

Since the Everglades exchange has been bugged since 1971, no doubt, atop some dusty shelf on a reel of magnetic tape sat the recording of our voices. We wondered later what the spying government agents thought that night of our soft drink-poll.

Everyone around me complained about the heat, rain, humidity, bugs, and dangerous animals in the Everglades. Though, the alligators kept me on my toes, and the mosquitoes and fleas kept my legs swollen with a slew of fresh itchy lumps, and despite the swarming insects and occasional scorpion, snake or sticker plant, I enjoyed my personal nature. My sister and I traveled the length of Ken's development toting fishing poles. We walked up to where his real estate office had become a store for bait and other conveniences with the name *Anhinga*. If we managed to bum money from the parents, we bought shrimp and worms, but even without that, a net snagged plenty of minnows. Right from the tail and through the back, but not too far as to poke through the mouth or eyes, I hooked the tiny fish in hopes of catching the bigger ones.

We spent hours on the dock behind the house, kicking the barnacles with our swinging legs, waiting for a fish to get on the line. Alligators taking in sun from the opposite bank or floating down-stream became interwoven into the landscape, and life seemed like an endless, never-changing existence.

Reprinted from the *Everglades City Mullet Rapper*, May 2012

Go Out and Play

Saturday morning, cartoons played until lunch at our home in Ochopee. Afterward, I went and sat my eight-year-old self in front of the television.

"No more TV," said Mother. "Go out and play in the backyard."

I rose, walked onto the porch through a screen door, and then wandered around the yard. Lying at the edge of the lawn was my bicycle.

Over the loose gravel, sparse grass, and sticker plants, I traveled a quarter of a mile around a canal and down a rugged trail. It led out beyond moon-crater-like rock pits. In the center of the narrowing path, shallow water collected and contained something white. Half submerged, an alligator skull with a hole in the top, stared from hallow sockets.

Thirty minutes later, a mound of quarry-blasted limestone loomed fifteen feet high and twenty-five square feet around. I leaped from my bike to go and climb but stopped short. A sun-bathing diamond-back rattle snake made its claim.

Continuing, I noticed movement in a pool to the side of the trail and brought my ride up to the rim. Little black pebbles or raisins or Mexican jumping beans shook, as if being boiled. I kneeled down and touched one: *bugs*.

In an hour, the terrain roughened, and the path ended. I kicked a rock, and a tiny scorpion ran around in a circle. I scanned the distant plains, eyeing their sharp golden saw grass and scattered lakes. With a shuffle and turn of the bike, I faced the way I came.

"You were out there awhile; you must have been busy," said Mother as I tromped through the kitchen. She shut the glass door and spotted an alligator skull placed on a table. She looked at me with a puzzled expression.

One night in early 1979, decked out in my pajamas, I ran past the front double doors of our house, and into the kitchen to get a bedtime glass of water. A banging on the front door startled me, and so I crept back to the corner to take a look. After more knocking, Dad opened the doors and I heard a stranger's voice. A man dressed in a uniform and carrying some papers handed them to Dad. The two exchanged a short argument that ended with Dad slamming the door. I dropped back into the kitchen, took the water, and rushed up the stairs to bed.

A few weeks later, I found out the reason for the visit, when Mom and Dad sat me down on the couch in the living room and said that we might have to move. I felt anxiety rise to the top of my head, and I asked them where. When they said we were headed out of the Everglades, I did not believe them, and I told them, "I'm not going."

Later, when evidence of the moving appeared in their plans of packing and talking about a new place, I began dealing with the facts. I curled up on the couch and began crying, protesting through my tears that I was not going to leave. That year, depression filled my days, and I tried to return to the favorite spots along the canal, the remote hangouts on the biking trails, and the dock, but nothing felt the same. I heard of the court cases and meetings and the fight to keep the motel, and I tried to learn the reason why we had to leave. From what I discerned, the government was to blame. I felt anger, and when the family invited me to the court hearings and meetings, I readied myself to go and yell at them all. At the last minute, I backed out, went and sat in my room, and stared through the two-story window over the swamp at the palm trees swaying in the wind.

1980. On the last day of school, I took a picture of my classmates while they stood around the jungle gym on the playground at Everglades City School. Many became friends through the Cub Scout organization that mom started in 1977. In just a few years, we had managed so much fun together.

With the truck pulling Dad's Airstream trailer, I sat with my sister and brother in the back seat. The truck pulled onto US 41 and started toward Naples. I thought about the whole life in the Everglades and all of the time spent, the people met, the animals, and the place I belonged to that made me who I was. I started crying and didn't stop for miles, and then began again for miles after that. I cried sometimes years later.

By age sixteen, I had adjusted to a new life near Tampa, Florida, in a small town called Brandon. I loved the big oak trees, where I climbed at will, and the thick grasses without stickers, but I never stopped thinking about Ochopee. That year, Mom, my siblings, and I took a trip in an old Ford motor home that my grandfather gave to Dad. The National Park Service let us go inside of our old "Pizza Hut" house, and I went up-stairs to my bedroom. Two guys sat behind desks where my bed used to be. They both wore suits with ties, and their big phones rested on the desk with wires going everywhere. I looked all around the room at the shelves, the papers, the books, and the place I had picked out in the blueprints. I gritted my teeth and felt angry. I wanted to do something. I wanted to, but I did not know what to do. Two years after that, I started researching to find out the reason why we had to leave and what happened to Ochopee.

JEANIE

Jeanie gathered her looks from the mirror and gazed at the new dress she had bought months ago, but had never worn. After a little more makeup and hair primping, she walked to the living room where her husband lay sprawled out on the couch. A mixed drink rested on a side table next to a bottle of Jack Daniels.

"Let's go out. We never see our friends anymore," she said to him.

"I am not going out. I'm watching the race." Engines blasted from the television with each car that rounded the track.

"You always watch that. Come on; let's get out of the house."

"No!" yelled her husband, "why don't you go play some cards or something."

"Well, I'm going to go alone then."

The man rose up from his spot and stood, looking at her. She saw anger swelling up in his eyes.

"You're not going anywhere. Go in the kitchen and make some food for the race."

"No, I want to go," said Jeanie as she headed for the front door.

"Where are you going?" he said.

"I'm just going down to our bar to meet our friends."

"The hell you are." He moved around the couch and up close to her. Jeanie felt his heaving and liquored breath. Her hand reached for the door knob, and his fist smashed her face.

Jeanie woke up and held tight to her fishing pole that rested in her hands. The violent image faded and gave way to the line running out and into the water. With the reel locked in place, she cranked the handle to reverse its direction. She sat up in her lawn chair on the dock behind her house and pulled against the force on the end of the pole. She turned the crank until a fish on the line emerged from the water.

"Hello, snook," said Jeanie. She brought the fish to the dock and secured it with her foot while she used pliers to remove the hook. With it out, she held the fish tightly with two hands and dropped it into a white five-gallon bucket. Still groggy from her nap, she lay back in her chair and rested.

It seemed so long ago, although really it was more of *so far away*, since she faced the abuses of her old husband. Clear across the other side of the country, deep in the Florida Everglades, she felt safe. In her twenties when they met, she remembered thinking five years ago how he had taken the best of her life. Now in her mid-thirties, she did not think that any longer. In Ohio, she met Ken Weimer, and just like in a story in a book, he picked her up and took her to his castle in the swamp-although the castle at first was a trailer and then a motel room for the first two years. He made good on his promise to build her a house. And *what a wonderful house*, she thought. She lifted up the bucket and looked at the fat fish, *her beautiful prize*. A glance at the sun told her that the time must be nearing six, and darkness was on the way. *No more sleeping*, she thought, *it's time to get to work*. She stood holding the bucket and went through the sliding glass doors to the house. The fish thudded on the cutting board. Taking a razor sharp-knife, she chopped off the tail and then cut across the neck of the fish on both sides. She then began to fillet the skin and scales from the body.

In the Everglades, isolated from civilization, she felt freer than she ever did with her old husband. Ken let her do whatever she wanted. He inspired her with his knowledge and raw determination, akin to a true pioneer. When they first met, she wondered how he could live in the swamp for all those decades, growing tomatoes and laying water lines. He never stopped working. Jeanie cut heavy slabs of meat from the sides of the fish and put them on a plate. *Really*, she thought, *he was never alone; he had his workers, but of course coming home every night to an empty trailer must have left him feeling empty. Well now, he has me.* She put the meat side by side in a pan with hot oil, and it sizzled. Salt and pepper she sprinkled over the fish, and then she took a glass from the cupboard. From the refrigerator, she brought out a bottle of white wine and filled the glass and then took a sip. Just as she was free to come and go as she pleased, so was Ken. Off to Frances Watson's home near her General

Store, he took along his bottle of liquor and sack of quarters. Over there, he would eat fresh blue crabs caught and steamed by Frances herself. Although alone for the night, she felt happy. Ken's native workers, his friends, he employed to build in their backyard one of their leaf-thatched structures called *chiki* by their language. Like an ancient primitive gazebo, the little hut in the grass near the dock overlooked the canal. Jeanie carried her finished dinner with glass of wine to a table and benches beneath the roof of the dwelling. Sitting inside, she faced west, and watched the falling sun drop behind the river of grass landscape. A mosquito buzzed her ear, and she swatted at it. In her mouth, she put a thick, white, flaky piece of fish and followed it with a sip of wine.

Jeanie Weimer in the Golden Lion diner 1975

Mop Up

RESOURCES

Justice for Land Use (JFLU)

For additional information about Ochopee's history and people and other projects related to abuses of land use, please go to this website: **JFLU.ORG**

Email: **goldenlionmi@aol.com**

Contact the author Jeff Whichello on Facebook or via email.

American Land Rights Association (ALRA)

To find help for your own personal land-use battles or to learn more about the history and current events relating to the topic, please go to this website: **LANDRIGHTS. ORG**

For immediate assistance with any questions, including legal options, please contact:

Chuck Cushman
Executive Director
American Land Rights Association
PO Box 400
Battle Ground, WA 98604
(360) 687-3087

Email: **ccushman@pacifier.com**
Facebook: facebook.com/www.landrights.org

The Golden Lion Motor Inn

Learn more about the Golden Lion from a book in the works at this website: **ALionintheSwamp.com**

Available on Netflix.com and for purchase through most merchandise outlets, watch the documentary called

Square Grouper, created by the Corbin Brothers. It details the beginning and history of the marijuana trade through the Everglades in the 1970s and 1980s.

Watch for a cameo of The Golden Lion Motor Inn in part three.

THE GOOD OF ALL, FOR THE COMMON GOOD, DEMOCRACY, AND FUTURE GENERATIONS

There is no such thing as "for the good of all." When someone uses this terminology it is being used as a technique for manipulation-it is a spell. For which good; for who, depends on the desire of the speaker. Some things for one person are not always good for another.

"For the Common Good," could apply to food, water, and shelter, which all life requires. Applying this concept to setting aside conservation sensitive land for exploration, study, and public use could be considered, but how is it good to remove a family's shelter or to lock up so much land under government control that people have no opportunity to live in the natural world?

Using the excuse, "this is democracy, not everyone is always going to agree," is a perversion of the use. Democracy is a standard where people vote and majority wins on a variety of topics. If the vote is to remove shelter from one of the voters against their will, than this is a clear violation of human rights. At the very least human rights trumps democracy, but in reality, the voters and any politicians hiding behind the legislation have not used democracy; they have used a twisted version of something closer to Nazism or Communism.

All people need shelter and the earth is the only shelter that they have been given. The earth cannot be saved for future generations. That is an abstract general concept, a figment of imagination, and an illusion. People who actually exist on earth need to worry for their own natural environment by keeping it clean and in order. When imaginary people arrive in the future, they will be responsible for keeping their natural world clean and free of pollution as well.

OCHOPEE

About the cover

The photo was sort of an accident. Every few years since when I lived in Ochopee I would take a photo of the two palm trees at the end of the canal. This is the place I saw many alligators when I came home from school in the afternoons. One year, long after moving away, I brought with me black and white film as well as color. I ran out of color so started shooting the other. I took the shot with no knowledge of the approaching storm, because the photo was taken in day light. Only the right palm tree remained, since the left one was taken out by a hurricane. To the left of the tree are the buildings created by Ken Weimer and Forrest Harmon for their water companies. All of the land shown in the photo was Ken Weimer's development, Everglade Shores, facing south, towards the end of Florida.

Ochopee was never a place for locals, but for pioneers, many not from Florida. People contributed to the community in their own way but their common goal was peace and prosperity. The following businesses continue to struggle under the oppression of government regulations. These last hold-outs need the help of their fellow citizens to keep what's left of the community alive. Take time to help support their unique American way of life. They are only partly free to pursue their happiness.

Please see the map at the front of the book for locations of these businesses:

TRAIL LAKES CAMPGROUND AND SKUNK APE RESEARCH CENTER

40904 Tamiami Trail
Ochopee, FL 34141
(239) 695-2275

http://www.skunkape.info

- Tent Camping
- RV Camping
- Swamp Bungalow Cabin
- Gift Shop
- Wildlife Exhibit

They are located on Highway 41 in Ochopee, Florida, fifteen miles south of Interstate 75 (old Alligator Alley), then four miles east of Highway 29. They are 36 miles east of Naples, 60 miles west of Miami and just 90 minutes from either the Miami International or Regional Southwest Florida International Airports.

They are close to all Florida Everglades activities including hiking, bird watching, canoeing, kayaking, fishing, and hunting.

Don't miss this unique experience. David Shealy has been around and he will teach you about things that you never thought to think. He's the legend of this swamp, not just because he's eccentric or knowledgeable, though he's all that and more, the real reason he is a legend can be heard in a song with the lyrics: *a country boy can survive.*

EVERGLADES ADVENTURE TOURS

40904 Tamiami Trail
Ochopee, FL 34141
(800) 504-6554

http://www.evergladesadventuretours.com

- Pole boat eco tours
- Kayak tours
- canoe tours
- Paddleboard Safaris
- Swamp hikes
- Gladesmen and Folk life Tour
- Day Safari Tour
- Group Tours
- Guided Fishing Tours

Trip Advisor rated 5 out of 5 stars

There's no comparision anywhere in Florida to what David Shealy's son Jack can provide for an unforgettable Everglades experience. He is owner and operator at Everglades Adventure Tours. He goes by "Little Jack" since his uncle is also named Jack. The newest edition to the family is his son, Turner.

Each Shealy family member possesses knowledge and skills passed down through their unique gladesman culture. These modern day pioneers provide visitors with accurate teachings pertaining to swamp survial, construction techniques, and animal and plant biology. A visit to the Everglades can only be complete by stopping by the Shealy camp.

WOOTEN'S FAMOUS AIRBOATS

32330 Tamiami Trail East
Ochopee, FL 34141
(800) 282-2781
(239) 695-2781

http://www.wootenseverglades.com

In business since 1953
9:00 a.m. - 4:30 p.m.
7 Days a Week

- Airboat rides
- Swamp Buggy Tours
- Animal sanctuary
- Live Alligator Show
- Extensive Gift shop
- Alligator farm with over 100 animals

Raymond Wooten perfected the airboat ride so everyone could share his vision and love of the wild Everglades nature. This adventure is a once in a life time event.

The Swamp Buggy Tour Located on the North Side of the property takes you slowly through the grasslands prairie, by an old Indian campsite, and into a dense and lush Cypress Swamp. Exotic foliage abounds, and you never know what may be around the next bend. In the fall and winter months, nesting Bald Eagle and Manatee sightings are often observed.

2013, the Wooten family sold the business to the Patel family after running it for sixty years. The new owners are young and full of energy and are putting the life back into Raymond's dream.

JOANIE'S BLUE CRAB CAFE

39395 U.S. HWY. 41
Ochopee, FL, 34141
(239) 695 2682

http://joaniesbluecrabcafe.com

- Great food
- Live entertainment daily
- Cold Beer

If the Golden Lion were around still, the food would have been the best in Ochopee, but since it's not, the only single other option is Joanie's place. Started in 1979, plenty of articles have been written about this hideaway in the boondocks. After a long day of hiking, canoeing, and seeing the grand land, this little red shack will allow you to relax, regroup and reflect on your travels. They are especially keen on their biker customers.

Check the internet website for a menu, and information about this business.

NATURE'S EXOTIC BEAUTY PHOTOGRAPHY AT LUCKY'S EVERGLADES OUTPOST

HC61 Box 67 Loop Road
Ochopee, FL 34141
(305) 525-1419
(239) 695-2550

luckyland@earthlink.net

- Personal photography
- Weekend festivities

Lucky's operation sits on the far eastern side of Ochopee, west of the Miccosukee Indian Reservation. He shoots his unique photography in his studio (The Everglades itself) by places his clients in distinct and exciting settings.

On weekends Lucky opens his gates to the public as he offers up hamburgers, hot-dogs, and cold refreshments amongst his unique collectible yard sale. Biker customers are always welcome.

Look for the red mailbox and the Lucky Strike sign. From the east end of Loop road it's 7.5 miles, and from the west end it's 16.5 miles.

Driving Directions:

From the West - From intersection of CR 29 and US 41, travel 37 miles east to Loop Road and make a right. Lucky's is 7.5 miles in, on the right. Or, travel 17 miles and enter Loop road from the unpaved end (at Monroe Station) and travel 16.5 miles to the Outpost, on the left.

From the East - From intersection of Krome Ave. and U.S. 41, travel 21 miles west to Loop road and make a left. Lucky's is 7.5 miles in, on the right.

GPS Coordinates:
N 25 45.017
W 80 56.163

THE OCHOPEE POST OFFICE

38000 Tamiami TRL E
Ochopee, FL 34141-2003
239-695-4131

Can a post office be a roadside attraction? Yes it can if it's Ochopee's post office. This little 7' x 8' shed is famous and it is faces challenges of its own to stay in business. A customer used to be able to walk into this post office and address the Post Master but with modern technology, it is filled to the brim with electronic machines.

Now that you know the history of this little shed and Ochopee itself, please take time to visit and see what is left of the community started by dreamers and visionaries. James Gaunt and Ralph Brown would be proud to see you there.

EVERGLADES CITY
OUTDOOR RESORTS

150 Smallwood Drive
Chokoloskee, FL 34138
239-695-2881
239-695-3338

orachokoloskee@aol.com

- RV Resort
- Motel
- Marina
- Fishing
- Canoe/Kayak

First priority, visit Ochopee but the adventure does not end there by a long shot. Turn left at the flashing light going west at CR 29. At the end of this road lies an island. Everglades City has around 300 residents and you might spend a week exploring it but before that happens do yourself the favor of visiting Outdoor Resorts. Take the south road from Everglades City to Chokoloskee. On this smaller island you will find the Brown family-an original founder. They will provide the insider tour that you could never get with the National Park Service option.

Founded in the 1800s this region is full of history. Find your way to the Smallwood Museum store in Chokoloskee. The place is a huge old building on stilts built long ago for trading between natives and settlers. It is full of ancient artifacts and hidden mysteries. It is also the site of Peter Matthiessen's book, *Killing Mister Watson*.

THANKS AND ACKNOWLEDGMENT

Thanks to these direct contributors

- Jeanie Weimer
- The Whichello Family
- The Wooten Family
- The Shealy Family
- Glenda Hancock
- George Hamilton
- Joe B. Browder
- Chuck Cushman
- Toby Prince Brigham
- Joann Watson
- Virginia Cougar
- Margie Weeks
- Kathy Williams Doster
- Midge Lessor
- Charles Knight
- Ralph E. Brown
- Alicia Marie Campanella

Additional thanks for inspiration and support

- Ray Dunkle
- Chris Richert

- Lucky Cole
- Cuco's Mexican Restaurant in Montgomery, Alabama
- Dana Monte of Alabama
- Patricia Sissey Mcleod of Alabama
- Jeanie from Billy D's
- Linda who brings flowers
- Christin Haynes of Alabama
- Donna Davis Pounders
- Barbara Stamper Wooten
- Brenda Keahey, Deanna, Nate, and Jake
- Floyd Brown
- Terri Griffin Rementeria
- Joanie Griffin
- The Daffin family
- Betty Brown Campbell
- Danny Sylvest
- Daniel Jenkins of Georgia
- Laila Milanian of Queens, NYC
- Leonard Silvenis of Michigan
- The Bennett family
- Irian Rodriguez of Pennsylvania

Special Thanks to

- **Jeanie Weimer**
  Thank you for putting up with the abuses of the land acquisition and for reconnecting after many years to answer so many questions. You passed away before the story finished, but without you this book would not be possible. Thank you for your total support of having our side of the story told: the people's side.

- **Frank Denninger**
  A real life super hero fighting for all of our freedoms from his remote swamp fortress of solitude

- **Jack Zatz aka Monk**
  A seasoned warrior in the war for human rights against government land abuse in Ochopee. You took some of the greatest wounds fighting back against oppression as you told the truth about the takeover of the land. You're one of the last living eye-witnesses and I thank you greatly for the knowledge and service you provided. Almost every day the proof arises in the media showing that the park system and all of the government agencies have too much power and are way out of control. Even now they are working to remove all private airboat use. Monk, your story I will make sure lives on in mine, because we share the same one.

- **Alvin Lederer**
  For years of encouragement, wise words, and great pictures, you never gave up on me and the importance of preserving history in the wake of uncaring government and environmental groups. So when are we going to actually meet? Hmm, it's 2018, and we still haven't met.

- **Jack, David, and Little Jack Shealy**
  For decades of friendship and goodwill and for decades to come; thank you for keeping alive the fight for our American freedom to live the way we want, whether bad or good, it's our choice given to us by the people who lost their lives to make this country a place of independent and individual thought and not a place coerced by over-lording government agencies or blinded, thoughtless environment groups with their inhuman agendas.

- **Pedro Ramos and Bob Degross**
  Thank you for letting Dad and I visit the Golden Lion one last time. Bob, thank you for your work on Monroe Station.

- **Joe Browder**

  Like Jeanie, the book would have not been near the same without your help Joe. Unlike Jeanie you were able to read the story before you passed.

  Though Joe was on the opposing team to protect the people of the Big Cypress, he did fight to make it a preserve rather than a national park which meant that at least people had *some* say so at the time. He said that the environmentalists had basically become so hard core nowadays that they no longer accepted his views. They alienated him.

  In our life we live in ruts and we are kept on their paths. Seldom does a person pull out of them and look above the clouds. It's when we do that that we are off track and then anything is possible. Staying in the ruts, you will one day just vanish without accomplishment. When you feel comfortable in your day to day existence with predictability and the time passes with nothing to show for it, then you are in a rut. Joe made sure he stayed out of them and so he accomplished much.

- **Patty Huff and Marya Repko**

  For giving Ochopee a chance to return in stories through the Mullet Rapper local newspaper and for helping me with wonderful advice and really I am thankful that you are preserving the history of Everglades City and the surrounding areas. I just hope Everglades City itself continues to produce history rather than to disappear like Ochopee. Everyone there feels there is something not right. The NPS has already started with the regulations and rules and direct competition with local businesses.

- **Maureen Sullivan-Hartung (writer:Hidden History of EG City)**

  For much help with book promotion. You are so wonderful!
  I highly suggest readers check out her book on Amazon.com.

- **April (sister)**

  If it wasn't for you, I would have been so alone in the swamp.

- **Andy (brother)**
  Thank you for coming with me on the trips to the Everglades. I wish Leebo's was still around.

- **John, Ed, Nancy, Patty, and Kathy**
  The musketeers that built the Golden Lion and helped create a wonderful community with creativity and hard work.

- **Daniel and Marge Whichello**
  For raising us kids in the beauty of the Everglades, an experience no longer possible. And for daring to live the American dream, though it was taken away. At least you tried when most never do.

- **Harlan Whichello**
  For trying to make sure your children found success though it was taken away. Your generation possessed a pioneering spirit that seemed lost in today's world.

- **Kelly Jennings Whichello**
  It has been my honor to have loved you and I always will. Your heart is one of the golden ones.

- **For People**
  Because how can we appreciate nature if we don't appreciate ourselves.

LOSING OCHOPEE

It's just us now - I human,
And you, a plethora of life forces,
The only real immortality
The magic and lore of real freedom, stolen
A quiet reincarnation each moment,
The way you sway tirelessly, a vast golden horizon
A resurrection borne of water and fire
Natural laws rewritten by the politics of greed.

Human lives pass without consequence
Like dragonflies in their tireless circumnavigation
In the backdrop of the saw grass,
A perpetual horizon of absolution and truth
Life and death unnoticed.

Holographic portraits, human stories, erased
Ghostlike in its wake,
The rhetoric and policy of a once living ghost town,
While paradox juxtaposes paradox,
We are, absorbed by a life force
Whose history we can hold but cannot carry
Fading in my rear view,
The shadows of a silenced history consuming you.

By Alicia Marie Campanella

Alicia Campanella is a writer, photographer and consulting forester. She worked at Fakahatchee Strand for several years where she created a program that helped identify invasive species priorities. Before working at Fakahatchee, Alicia completed a reforestation program in the Amazon, at Ecuador's Jatun Sacha Biological Reserve. She is keenly interested in local history and an integral part of Ochopee today, living and working there.

SOURCES

Balance
- "Ochopee: the Story of the Smallest Post Office," Maria Stone, 1989

People First
Jeanie's poem
- Interview with Jeanie Weimer, 2009
- "Ochopee: the Story of the Smallest Post Office," Maria Stone, 1989

Something from Nothing
- "Ochopee: the Story of the Smallest Post Office," Maria Stone, 1989
- Letter from Ralph E. Brown, March 7, 2014

Weimer
- Interviews with John Whichello, Nancy Whichello, Margaret Schleif-Whichello and Daniel Whichello
- Interview with Jeanie Weimer, 2009
- Google.com maps
- Author memory

Wooten
- Interview with Shelly Wooten, 2013
- Interview with Gene Wooten, 2013
- *Naples Daily News*, "Sunniland Oil History," Katherine Albers, April 2, 2012
- Chapter Review by Richard Wooten, 2013

- Chapter Review by Barbara Stamper Wooten, 2013
- Interview with Kimberly Wooten, 2013

Shealy

- Interviews with David and Jack Shealy, 2013
- *Everglades Skunk Ape Research Field Guide*, David Shealy
- Interview with Daniel and Marge Whichello
- Author memory

The Smallest Post Office

- *"Ochopee: the Story of the Smallest Post Office,"* Maria Stone, 1989
- Letter from Ralph E. Brown, March 7, 2014

Harmon

- Interview with Midge Lessor, 2008, 2013
- Interviews with Daniel Whichello, John Whichello, Nancy Whichello, and Margaret Schleif-Whichello
- Author memory

Watson

- Author purchased T-shirt from Ma Watson's store
- Interview with Joann Watson, 2013
- Author memory
- Interview with anonymous hunter, 2012
- Newspaper clipping from Virginia Cougar
- Letter from Ralph E. Brown, March 7, 2014

Whichello

- Interviews with Daniel, Ed, John, Nancy, Patty, Kathy Whichello and Margaret Schleif-Whichello, 2013
- Author memory
- *The Craftsman*, "A Success Story," Henry Ford Trade School newspaper, 1945

Takers
Conflict of Interest
- *The Herald-Tribune*, the Associated Press, 1969
- *The Swamp*, Michael Grunwald, 2006
- Interview with Joe Browder, 2013
- Inauguration video of President Richard M. Nixon, 1969
- Chapter review by Joe Browder, 2013

Big Cypress Swamp
- *Lakeland Ledger*, "Nixon Proposes Congress Buy Big Cypress Swamp," the Associated Press, November 24, 1971
- Interview with Joe Browder, 2013
- Interview with Daniel Whichello, 2013

Miami Hearing
- *The Palm Beach Post*, "Big Cypress, a Chance to Gripe," Susan Hixon post staff writer, December 1, 1971
- Interview with Daniel Whichello, eyewitness
- *St. Petersburg Times*, "Cypress Called a Pawn," Mike Toner – *Times-Miami Herald* Service, November 26, 1971
- *Sarasota Herald-Tribune*, "Former Governor Bucks Big Cypress Purchase," the Associated Press, Decembeer 1, 1971

Preparing for War
- *Lakeland Ledger*, "Nixon Proposes Congress Buy Big Cypress Swamp," the Associated Press, November 24, 1971
- *Naples Daily News*, "Big Cypress Landowners Prepare for Legal Fight," Dollie Gull, staff writer, December 12, 1971
- *Ocala Star Banner*, "Politics or not, Acquiring Big Swamp is a Good Idea," November 29, 1971
- "A. C. Hancock," Glenda Hancock

Devalue

- *Miami News,* "Congress Gets Bill to Buy 547,000 acres of Big Cypress," the Associated Press, February 8, 1972
- *St. Petersburg Times,* "Askew Urges U.S. State Effort to Save Swamp," Times Wire Service, April 21, 1972
- *St. Petersburg Times,* "Askew Move May Save Big Cypress," Reg Crowder staff writer, April 6, 1973
- *St. Petersburg Times,* "Big Cypress Funds Approved by Senate," June 1, 1973
- *Boca Raton News,* "Askew, Cabinet Hear Big Cypress Debate," November 14, 1973
- *St. Petersburg Times,* "Big Cypress One Battle in War Over Land Rights," Jere Moore, Jr., November 12, 1973
- *Daytona Beach Public Journal,* "Public is Heard on Cypress," November 14, 1973
- *Sarasota Herald-Tribune,* "Property Rights Battle Forming around Big Cypress Watershed," Allan Horton Herald-Tribune staff writer, November 15, 1973
- *Dayton Beach Morning Journal,* "Big Cypress Controversy Mounts," John Mueller, October 28, 1973 (Rhodes interview)
- *Naples Daily News,* "Walker Stands by Statement," Mary Ellen Hawkins, September 28, 1973
- *St. Petersburg Times,* "Conservation Award to Shevin," September 8, 1973
- *St. Petersburg Times,* "Session on Big Cypress Unruly," September 8, 1973
- Interview with Earl Starnes, 2012
- Interview with Joe Browder, 2013
- Florida Memory, http://www.floridamemory.com/collections/governors/florida-cabinet.php

Saving Ochopee

- *Naples Daily News,* "Ochopee Acquisition Appeal Made," Frank Pettengill, staff writer, July 23, 1975

- *Naples Daily News*, "County Told to go ahead with plans for Ochopee," Frank Pettengill, staff writer, July 29, 1975
- *Naples Daily News*, "Future of Ochopee Concerns Commissioners," Frank Pettengill, staff writer, August 19, 1975
- *Naples Daily News*, "County Hopes for Aid to Offset Land Loss," Frank Pettengill, staff writer, July 29, 1975
- Watergate Scandal, Wikipedia, http://en.wikipedia.org/wiki/Watergate_scandal

Oil

- *St. Petersburg Times*, "Cabinet Okays Test Oil Wells in Big Cypress Swamp," the Associated Press, May 4, 1976
- Interview with Daniel Whichello, eye witness
- *Naples Daily News*, "Big Cypress Draws Oil Explorers," the Associated Press, May 3, 1976
- *The Village Voice*, "The Florida Story," Mark Jacobson, May 29, 1978

Land Commissions

- Interview with Toby Prince Brigham, 2010
- Wikipedia, http://en.wikipedia.org/wiki/Fifth_Amendment_to_the_United_States_Constitution
- Interview with Daniel Whichello eyewitness, 2013

NPS and ALRA

- History of the Interior, interior.gov/whoweare/history.cfm
  nps.gov/aboutus/history.htm
  nps.gov/yose/planyourvisit/wildpermits.htm
- *National Inholder News*, Vol.3 No.5, May 1980
- *National Inholder News*, Vol.3 No.6, July-August 1980
- Interview with Chuck Cushing, 2013

GAO
- TheFreeDictionary.com
- Report by the Comptroller General of the United States, "The Federal Drive to Acquire Private Lands Should be Reassessed."
- National Park Inholders Association Newsletter, September/October, 1980
- National Park Inholders Association Newsletter, November 1980
- National Inholders Association letter to Honorable James McClure Chairman Appropriations Interior Subcommittee, Charles S. Cushman, March 26,1981
- *Sarasota Herald-Tribune*, "U.S. Reassures Graham of Big Cypress Purchase," Sam Miller, June 20, 1981

Ohio
- *Front Line* television special, "For the Good of All," produced and directed independently by Mark and Dan Jury, produced by Stephanie Kepper

Simple Life
The Bowling Ball German shepherd
- Interview with Daniel and Marge Whichello
- Interview with John Whichello

Golden Lion
- Interview with Margie Weeks
- Interview with Daniel and Nancy Whichello

Dry Season
- Interviews with Nancy Whichello, Kathy Whichello, Daniel Whichello, eyewitnesses
- *The Palm Beach Post*, "Two Fires Devouring Big Cypress Swamps," May 31, 1973

The Hog
- Interview with hunter, personal account, Sonny, 2011 (Name changed to protect source)

The Cabin
- Interview with hunter, personal account, Milo, 2013 (Name changed to protect source)

David Carradine
- *St. Petersburg Times*, Fred W. Wright Jr., 1977
- *Naples Daily News*, Allen Bartlett, 1977
- Internet Movie Database, IMDB.com
- Pictures of David Carradine by Daniel Whichello, 1977
- Interview with Kathy Williams Doster
- Interview with Jeanie Weimer, 2009
- Interview with Marge Whichello

Ochopee Scouts
- Author memory

Daniel
- Interview with Daniel Whichello
- Interview with Jack Shealy
- Interview with Nancy Whichello

Mother vs. Nature
- Author memory
- Interview with Marge Whichello

The Bar
- Interview with Daniel, Nancy, and Ed Whichello
- Interview with Malcolm Smith at Leebo's Bar
- Charles Knight

Casualties

The Monday Morning Rumor Association

- Interview with Daniel Whichello, eyewitness
- *The Village Voice*, "The Florida Story," Mark Jacobson, May 29, 1978

Whichello

- Interview with eyewitness at the sheriff auction, 2013
- *The Tampa Tribune*, "U.S. Vows to Acquire 90% of Big Cypress," June 20, 1981
- www.gpo.gov/fdsys/pkg/STATUTE-84/pdf/STATUTE-84-Pg1894.pdf
- www.gpo.gov/fdsys/pkg/STATUTE-88/pdf/STATUTE-88-Pg1258.pdf
- Interview with John Whichello, 2012
- Letters from David J. Buchanan, Environmental Specialist, July 15, 1977, July 18, 1977, August 12, 1977, August 15, 1977
- Letters from James F. Sewell, Land Acquisition Officer, July 18, 1977, August 3, 1977, August 19th, 1977
- Letter from Bill Gunter, State Treasurer and Insurance Commissioner, August 1, 1977
- Letter from Bruce A. Smathers, Secretary of State of Florida, August 8, 1977
- Letter from Gerald A. Lewis, Comptroller of the Department of Banking and Finance of the State of Florida, August 8, 1977
- Letter from Harmon Shields, Executive Director of the state of Florida of National Resources, August 12, 1977, August 15, 1977
- Letter from Robert L. Shevin, Attorney General of Florida, August 12, 1977
- Letter from Andy Ireland, Congress 8th district of Florida, August 15, 1977
- Letter from Florida Governor O'D. Askew, August 16, 1977

Watson

- *Naples Daily News*, "Appraisal Action Begins in Ochopee," Frank Pettengill, 4/23/1976

- *Naples Daily News*, "Big Cypress Draws Oil Explorers," the Associated Press, May 3, 1976
- *Naples Daily News*, "Sad Day for Ochopee: Mrs. Watson Sells Out," Steve Herendeen, county reporter, August 25, 1976
- Interview with Joann Watson, 2009, 2013

Harmon
- *St. Petersburg Times*, David Conyers, November 4, 1986
- Interview with Daniel Whichello
- Interview with Midge Lessor, 2013

Gaunt's Post Office
- Interview with Daniel Whichello who knew Gaunt well
- The Lion's Club History, http://www.lionsclubs.org/EN/about-lions/mission-and-history/our-history/lions-history-hkspeech.php, page 60
- "Remembering Ochopee," Erica Lynne, 1995
- "Ochopee: the Story of the Smallest Post Office," Maria Stone, 1989

Shealy
- Interview with Jack Shealy
- Interview with David Shealy
- Chapter Review by Frank Denninger
- "Part of Tamiami Trail awarded Scenic Highway Status," NaplesNews.com, 1999
  http://web.naplesnews.com/special/skunkape/trailjan.htm
- *U.S. Department of Transportation Office of Public Affairs News release*, 2000
  http://www.fhwa.dot.gov/pressroom/fhwa0042.cfm
- *Naples Daily News*, "Tamiami Trail Designation as a Scenic Byway," http://www.naplesnews.com/news/2006/oct/04/877dbb99d456f948ab91fe2eac33e15a/
  2005
- The native official public response to the government

Wooten
- Chapter review by Barbara Stamper Wooten
- Chapter review by Richard Wooten
- Chapter review by Kimberly Wooten
- Chapter review by Tina Wooten
- Chapter review by Shelly Wooten
- Picture credits: Kimberly, Tina Wooten
- Picture credit: Google Maps
- *Miami Herald*, "Iconic airboats won't be part of Everglades culture for much longer", Sue Cocking, December 27, 2013

Weimer
- Interview with Jeanie Weimer, 2009
- Interview with Daniel and Marge Whichello

A Kid in the Swamp
- Author memory

Jeanie
- Interview with Jeanie Weimer, 2009

Made in the
USA
Columbia, SC